TABLE OF CONTENTS

Volume 4: 1 and 2 Samuel

by Donald W. Dotterer
James A. Durlesser
C. Stephen Byrum

Art and Photo Credits: p. 15, John Ham; p. 40, photo by J. A. Durlesser. From the exhibit at the James L. Kelso Bible Lands Museum, Pittsburgh Theological Seminary, Pittsburgh, Pennsylvania. Used by permission; p. 57, © 1981 Biblical Archaeology Society.

$\mathcal{I}$NTRODUCTION TO THE SERIES

Welcome to JOURNEY THROUGH THE BIBLE!
You are about to embark on an adventure that can change your life.

WHAT TO BRING WITH YOU
Don't worry about packing much for your trip. All you need to bring with
you on this journey are
- an openness to God speaking to you in the words of Scripture
- companions to join you on the way, and
- your Bible

ITINERARY
In each session of this volume of JOURNEY THROUGH THE BIBLE, first you
will be offered some hints for what to look for as you read the Bible text,
and then you will be guided through four "dimensions" of study. Each is
intended to help you through a well-rounded appreciation and application
of the Bible's words.

HOW TO PREPARE FOR YOUR JOURNEY THROUGH THE BIBLE
Although you will gain much if all you do is show up for Bible study and par-
ticipate willingly in the session, you can do a few things to gain even more:
- Read in advance the Bible passage mentioned in What to Watch For,
using the summaries and hints as you read.
- During your Bible reading, answer the questions in Dimension 1.
- Read the rest of the lesson in this study book.
- Try a daily discipline of reading the Bible passages suggested in
Dimension 4. Note that the Bible texts listed in Dimension 4 do *not* relate
to a particular lesson. But if you continue with this daily discipline, by the
end of thirteen weeks, you will have read through *all* of that portion of the
Bible covered by this volume.

Studying the Bible is a lifelong project. JOURNEY THROUGH THE BIBLE provides you with a guided tour for a few of the steps along your way. May
God be with you on your journey!

Gary I. Ball-Kilbourne
Executive Editor, Adult Publications
Church School Publications

Questions or comments?
Call Curric-U-Phone 1-800-251-8591.

1 Samuel 1; 3

A GIFT TO GOD

What to Watch For

First Samuel includes the story of the birth and childhood of Samuel, a man who would become a new and different kind of leader for Israel. Chapter 1 tells about the unusual circumstances of Samuel's birth. Pay close attention to the cultural expectations of women with regard to children and family. Note the rivalry between Hannah and her husband's other wife. Note too that through the experience of prayer and faith, Hannah is able to move from bitterness to joy and to give her son to God as an expression of her gratitude.

Chapter 3 tells of how God called the boy Samuel. Why did God need to call three times? What was the role of Eli as Samuel's mentor and friend? Note the close relationship that Samuel had with God.

Dimension 1: What Does the Bible Say?

1. What was the cause of Hannah's distress? (1 Samuel 1:3-10)

2. What was Hannah's response to answered prayer? (1 Samuel 1:20-22)

3. What role did Eli play when God called Samuel? (1 Samuel 3:2-9)

4. What exactly did God say to Samuel when the boy finally answered the call? (1 Samuel 3:10-14)

Dimension 2: What Does the Bible Mean?

The books of Samuel describe a major transition in leadership for the covenant people of Israel. Times were changing, as we will see later in more detail. The confederation of tribes that was ruled by the judges in the land of Canaan was threatened by military pressure from their enemies to the west, the Philistines.

The Lord God, in infinite wisdom and concern for the well-being of the covenant people, moved to raise up a new and different kind of leader who would be able to meet the challenges of the new age, at least temporarily. This new leader would serve as prophet, priest, and judge until the Israelites would receive from God the appointment of a king to rule over them.

God's chosen leader was Samuel. From the beginning, we learn that God worked in a miraculous way to provide Israel with this unique leader.

The Birth and Dedication of Samuel

Elkanah (el-KAY-nuh) was a member of the increasingly prominent tribe of Ephraim (EE-fray-im), which had already established a glorious tradition within the history of Israel. The problem here was that Elkanah's favorite wife, Hannah, was unable to bear him a son.

In ancient Israel the worst disaster that could befall a woman was the inability to bear a son who would be an heir and carry on her husband's name. Since the Israelites had no conception of an afterlife in heaven, the way in which a man lived into the future was through children who would bear his name for future generations. We remember how Abraham's blessing from God included the promise that the covenant would be established between not only Abraham and God but also his "offspring" after him "throughout their generations" (Genesis 17:7).

In ancient Israel the worst disaster that could befall a woman was the inability to bear a son.

Elkanah had another wife, Peninnah (pi-NIN-uh), who did bear him children. Polygamy was not common among the Hebrews, but it was not prohibited. Having more than one wife was a kind of insurance policy so that a man would have a better chance of having heirs. Elkanah clearly favored Hannah, as he gave her a "double portion" of his sacrifices. This good and kind man sympathized with his beloved Hannah's pain and embarrassment but was unable to keep his second wife, described as "her rival," from taunting her.

In her distress Hannah went to the Israelite worship center at Shiloh. Here the tabernacle was set up and the ark of the covenant was located. The Hebrews thought that God was in complete control of everything that happened. They believed that God had the power to give or withhold children. So Hannah prayed fervently to God, so intensely that the priest Eli thought she had been drinking too much wine. With tears streaming down her face, she vowed that if God would grant her the gift of a son, she would dedicate him to the work of God. She would see that he became a nazirite, which means "dedicated" or "consecrated" one.

NAZIRITES

Nazirites were set apart to live a holy life, either for a lifetime or for a limited amount of time. There were three specific conditions: they were to refrain from drinking wine; from allowing their hair to be cut; and from touching dead bodies, even those of their father and mother. Men and women became nazirites through their own decision or by the choice of their parents. Samson was dedicated a nazirite while still in his mother's womb (Judges 13:2-5).

After receiving Eli's blessing, Hannah returned home and was at peace. Not long after this she conceived and bore a son whom she named Samuel, which means "name of God." In her joy Hannah gave added meaning to his name by saying, "I have asked him of the LORD" (1 Samuel 1:20). First Samuel 2 records Hannah's song of thanksgiving for answered prayer.

The circumstances of Samuel's conception are not unique in the Bible.

The birth of children to formerly barren women, usually late in life, occurred several times. These pregnancies were seen as special favors from God, and each of the children went on to play an important role in the history of Israel.

FORMERLY BARREN WOMEN WHO GAVE BIRTH TO GREAT LEADERS OF ISRAEL

Sarah	Isaac	Genesis 17:15-19
Rebekah	Jacob & Esau	Genesis 25:19-26
Rachel	Joseph	Genesis 30:22-24
Samson's mother	Samson	Judges 13:2-5, 24
Elizabeth	John the Baptist	Luke 1:5-17

God Calls Samuel

As Chapter 3 opens, we see that Samuel is no longer a young child. Hannah has kept her promise and has given her child to God. The Jewish historian Josephus places his age at twelve, which in the Jewish tradition was the time when a male child became a "son of the commandment." At this age the boy was held personally accountable for his obedience to the law of Moses. Jesus was twelve years of age when Mary and Joseph found him having discussions with the teachers of the Temple in Jerusalem, amazing them with "his understanding." Like Samuel, his "Father's house" was simply where Jesus had to be (Luke 2:40-51).

Why was it necessary for Samuel to learn the duties and responsibilities of the sanctuary? One of the reasons was that the priest Eli's own sons, who presumably should have inherited the work, had turned out to be scoundrels and good-for-nothings. We read that "Eli's sons were wicked men; they had no regard for the LORD" (1 Samuel 2:12, New International Version). These were not people who could be given the responsibility for the critically important work of caring for the house of God.

At twelve years of age, Samuel, like all Jewish boys, became a "son of the commandment."

Eli's sons, named Hophni (HOF-nigh) and Phinehas (FIN-ee-uhs), had mocked the law of God. They disregarded the strict and specific regulations governing the handling of sacrifices to God. Their work was sacred, and they had violated God's trust. In fact, their sin was so great that they would have to die.

For this reason God needed a different person to succeed Eli, a "faithful priest" who would do that which was in accordance with the heart and mind of God (1 Samuel 2:35). That chosen leader would be the boy Samuel.

We are told that "the word of the LORD was rare in those days" (1 Samuel 3:1b). The infrequency of God's direct revelation to humans added to the importance of God's call to Samuel. The mark of a true prophet throughout Scripture is one who has an especially close relationship with God and possesses the special ability to receive directly the "word of the LORD."

> The mark of a true prophet is one who has an especially close relationship with God and possesses the special ability to receive directly the "word of the LORD."

When Samuel heard a voice calling to him, it must have been near morning, since the night lamp ("the lamp of God," 3:3) was not permitted to go out until dawn. Note that not only Samuel but also Eli did not realize that this was God who was calling to Samuel until the voice had called three times.

The revelation to Samuel marks the beginning of his prophetic ministry, the point at which Samuel began to "know" God in a personal way. The content of God's message was disturbing; and Samuel was afraid to tell Eli that God would judge his family, with the implication that Samuel would be the new leader of the Hebrew people. However, Eli demonstrated that he was a man of great faith and simply accepted the judgment of God. From this point on, God was with Samuel; and Samuel was known and trusted as a genuine prophet of God.

Dimension 3:
What Does the Bible Mean to Us?

The Root of Our Anger

After a recent national election a majority of the voters described themselves as "dissatisfied" or "angry." What were they so angry about? Public opinion polls tell us that the voters' anger was due to their uncertainty about the future. People just do not know what the future will hold. They are afraid that they or their children will not be able to live as well as they have lived in the past. In other words, many people have given up hope for a better tomorrow. And this is what is really at the root of their anger.

> Many people are afraid that they or their children will not be able to live as well as they have lived in the past. So, they have given up hope for a better tomorrow.

This observation about angry voters can help us in understanding the story of Hannah and the birth and dedication of her son Samuel. First, we read that Hannah was a bitter woman. She was

7

bitter and "deeply distressed" in spite of the fact that she had many won-derful things in life. Hannah was loved and adored by her husband. He provided her with more material things than she needed. But despite all this, she was unhappy, envious, and bitter at the cards that life had dealt her.

What was the reason for Hannah's unhappiness and bitterness? She was distressed because she was unable to conceive a child. To be childless in ancient Israel was the worst thing that could happen to a woman. To be without children was to live a life without worth and meaning. Hannah's distress and bitterness was rooted in the fact that she was not able to pro-vide her husband with an heir; in other words, she was unable to provide him with a future.

Hannah had waited a long time for a child. And she did not need to be reminded of that by "her rival."

We too spend much of our time waiting for things to happen. We are convinced that some future event will occur that will solve some deep problems. Like Scarlett O'Hara in *Gone With the Wind*, we believe that "After all, tomorrow is another day." And we believe that that day will just have to be better.

But sometimes people have to wait too long. Sometimes we do not get what we want even if we wait a lifetime. Hannah believed her waiting might never end. She felt that there was hope but not for her. That is why she was so bitter, both at God and at the world.

Sometimes we feel like Hannah. We feel that there is hope but not for us. There is hope for others, but we have no reason to hope. We may feel that too many years have passed by to expect to have a better tomorrow. We may feel that too many opportunities have been lost. We may think that while others have had the good life dropped in their laps, life has just passed us by. We say, "Well, God, what about me? Where is my share? I want it now. I have waited just too long."

> We can call on a greater spiritual power when we need comfort and strength and help in time of trouble. All we need to do is to get down on our knees and pray. The peace and comfort of God will then come to us.

This must be how Hannah felt. She had a deep, aching emptiness in her heart that just would not go away. Life had not turned out the way she wanted it to be, and the future did not look any better. We have to respect Hannah, however, because she did what people should do when they are troubled. She went to pray in the house of God.

When she went to the worship center at Shiloh, Hannah prayed intensely. Tears streamed down her face. She prayed that if God would give her a son, she would give him back to God. She prayed this prayer so hard that the priest thought she had been drinking too much.

Hannah's story, of course, has a happy ending. She left the worship center with the priest's blessing and a sense of peace. Her prayer was answered. She fulfilled her promise and dedicated her son to the work of God.

Hannah's story is about the healing power of prayer. It is about the truth that there is a greater spiritual power we can call on when we need comfort and strength and help in time of trouble. All we need to do is to get down on our knees and pray. The peace and comfort of God will then come to us.

Called By God

Two aspects of Samuel's experience of God are helpful to us in our faith journey. First, we read that the boy Samuel did not know God before he was called; for "the word of the LORD had not yet been revealed to him" (1 Samuel 3:7). This suggests to us that although God takes the initiative in granting us the gift of faith, we need to be alert and aware to the possibility that God may be calling us. Our prayer life should be "active listening" as we wait for God to speak to us.

Second, note that God had to call Samuel three times before either he or Eli realized what was going on. How many times does God have to call us before we respond? Are we actively seeking God's will for our life through a disciplined study of God's holy word? If the word of God is "rare" in our time, could it be that we simply are not alert and ready to hear it? Is God calling us to take over ministry that other people cannot or will not do?

After Samuel answered the call, he began to grow in faith and ability. God "let none of his words fall to the ground," which means that Samuel's words were reliable and that he was trusted and respected by all the people (1 Samuel 3:19-20). Those who are called by God to leadership and who respond in faith gain strength and stature in the community. Just as God was with Samuel, so God will be with us when we seek to serve God with commitment and integrity.

> Just as God was with Samuel, so God will be with us when we seek to serve God with commitment and integrity.

In addition to the stature that Samuel gained among his people, we should also recognize the close relationship that Samuel developed with God. That relationship was the source of Samuel's strength and wisdom. So can it also be with us if we open our hearts and allow the Spirit of God to dwell within us.

Dimension 4:
A Daily Bible Journey Plan

Day 1: 1 Samuel 1

Day 2: 1 Samuel 2:1-17

Day 3: 1 Samuel 2:18-36

Day 4: 1 Samuel 3:1–4:1a

Day 5: 1 Samuel 4:1b-11

Day 6: 1 Samuel 4:12-22

Day 7: 1 Samuel 5

1 Samuel 4:1b-11; 5

2

GOD'S POWER OVER ALL PEOPLE

What to Watch For

This lesson is concerned with the beginning of the long and bloody struggle of the Israelites with their neighbors to the west, the Philistines (fi-LIS-teenz). This military threat and rivalry eventually led to Israel's need to unite under a king to defend themselves.

Read 1 Samuel 4:1b-11 and Chapter 5. In these passages the focus of attention shifts from the human character Samuel to an object, the ark of the covenant. The ark is captured by the enemy. Consider carefully the reasons why God would allow this to happen. The disaster that God said would befall the house of Eli (1 Samuel 3:12-14) comes to pass.

Note how this defeat shocks the Israelites and makes it clear to them that if they are not obedient to God, God will use their enemies to punish them. They learn that God cannot be contained or manipulated by humans. Also note what happens to the Philistines, who believe that they have won a great victory because of their superior god and military power.

Dimension 1: What Does the Bible Say?

1. What role does the ark of the covenant play in the life of Israel? (1 Samuel 4:2-3, 5-11)

2. How did the presence of the ark on the battlefield affect the Philistines? (1 Samuel 4:6-9)

3. What did the Philistines learn about the God of Israel in what they believed was a great military victory for them? (1 Samuel 5)

Dimension 2:
What Does the Bible Mean?

The beginning of Israel's war with the Philistines marks an important phase of Israel's history. The covenant people were about to learn some difficult lessons about what it meant to be a "chosen people." They must relearn the lesson that God and Moses taught them in the wilderness after their triumphant escape from slavery in Egypt: although God had chosen the Israelites and wanted to bless them, God demanded faith and obedience in return. These were the terms of the covenant that God made first with Abraham and then with Moses. If Israel failed in this department, which it would do over and over again throughout its history, then the people would not be exempted from defeat and disaster. Israel was a people chosen, not for special privilege, but rather for special responsibilities in relationship to God, the creator of all the peoples of the earth.

The War With the Philistines
The judge Samson had battled and defeated the Philistines but not until after he succumbed to the beauty of one of their women named Delilah (Judges 16). However, the mighty Samson's victory did not hold the Philistines at bay for long. During the time of Samuel, the Philistines became a real threat to the survival of the covenant people of God.

In this passage we find the Philistines initiating military action as they "mustered for war against Israel." This movement initiated Philistia's attempt to expand eastward into central Canaan, the area inhabited by the Israelite tribes. Their attempts at expansion would not be completely halted until King David defeated them once and for all.

Who were these Philistines? Unlike the other peoples whom the Israelites encountered in the land of Canaan, the Philistines were not of

Semitic origin, as were the Israelites. The Philistines had migrated from the Aegean Sea area in the early twelfth century B.C., eventually settling on what is now the southwest coast of Israel, including the Gaza area. Contrary to the popular usage of the word *philistine* to describe people who are crude and lacking in cultural and aesthetic values, the Philistines had a rich and highly developed civilization.

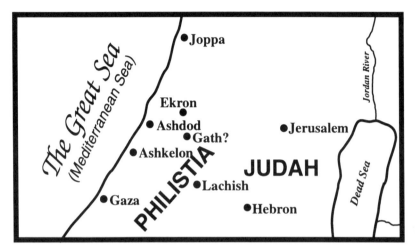

The Philistines were one of the nations that God had left in the Promised Land to "test" the Israelites, "who had no experience of any war in Canaan" (Judges 3:1-3). There was an established tradition of God working through pagan peoples to shape and discipline the Israelites. Remember how God "hardened Pharaoh's heart" so the Egyptian ruler would refuse to let the Hebrew people go free from slavery? Why? So that God could do "signs" that would make the Israelites know that God was God (Exodus 10:1-2).

The Ark of the Covenant

As the Philistines mount their attack on the Israelites, it is clear that they are the aggressors. They apparently had concluded that they were strong enough to defeat Israel and capture its territory. Note that Samuel is not a part of this narrative. The focal point is instead the ark of the covenant.

As the battle proceeded, Israel was thrashed by the Philistines, losing four thousand men. The elders wondered aloud, "Why has the LORD put us to rout today?" (1 Samuel 4:3). They could not believe that God's people could be so easily defeated by a pagan nation.

The Israelite elders concluded that they must be doing something wrong. They decided to bring the ark of the covenant from the worship center in Shiloh onto the battlefield. Hophni and Phineas, the wicked

13

WHAT WAS THE
ARK OF THE COVENANT?

The ark of the covenant was the most holy possession of the Hebrew people. It was a rectangular box made of acacia wood, measuring approximately 48x30x30 inches and overlaid with gold. This portable shrine was first kept in the holy of holies in the sanctuary of the tabernacle and later in the temple at Shiloh. Inside the chest were Israel's most sacred items—the stone tablets on which the law given to Moses was written, Aaron's rod that grew buds, and a golden urn containing manna from the Hebrews' wilderness experience.

The most significant characteristic of the ark was that it was identified with the presence of God. God, who lived in "the high and holy place," sat above the ark in a "mercy seat," or throne, invisibly present between two winged cherubim who stood guard. Therefore the Israelites believed that where the ark was located, so also was their God.

priests who were the sons of Eli, apparently approved of this action, as they are identified as the keepers of the ark.

The elders consented to have the ark carried into the heat of battle so that God would be with the men of Israel as they fought to repulse the onslaught of the Philistines. Israel gave a mighty shout, and the Philistines became afraid the god of the Hebrews would do the same thing to them that was done to the Egyptians.

However, the leaders of Israel made a serious error in judgment. The ark of the covenant was not intended to be used in such a manner. The inappropriate use of the ark was such a great sin that when Eli learned what had been done, he was so stunned that he fell backward and died (4:18). The old and devout judge obviously had a better understanding of the nature and purpose of the ark than did the elders or his sons.

The end result of this improper use of the ark was that the Israelites suffered a terrible defeat, losing thirty thousand men. Phineas and Hophni, the wicked priests who had allowed the ark to be brought into battle, met their death. (See the prediction of their death in 1 Samuel 2:34.) Worst of all, the Philistines took possession of the sacred ark of God.

What had gone wrong? First of all, Israel had sinned; and God was using the Philistines to discipline the covenant people. There is never any suggestion that God's people were defeated by a stronger foe. God instead used a pagan people to correct the Israelites because of their sin.

The elders had mistakenly assumed that God's presence was limited spatially to the ark. This was a theological error that God needed to cor-

Artist's conception of the ark of the covenant based on Exodus 25.

rect. God did so in a dramatic way, by allowing the unthinkable to happen—the capture of the ark by a pagan people. God may have been present with the ark in a special way; but God's presence was certainly not limited to any object, regardless of how much it was revered by the people. The elders' decision was outrageous in that they believed that God could be manipulated by human actions.

The Philistines Possess the Ark

The Philistines must have been elated by their great victory. They remembered how this god had troubled their other rivals, the Egyptians (4:8). They believed that their god Dagon (DAY-gon) had defeated this god, who was a formidable foe indeed.

However, their celebration was short-lived. The ark was placed in the temple of Dagon. But the next morning the statue of Dagon was found smashed on the ground in front of the ark. To the Philistines, their idol was their god. They did not make the distinction between image and spirit, which the Israelites were commanded to do in the second commandment (Exodus 20:4).

Then the real trouble began. The Philistines were struck with tumors, the painful boils of the bubonic plague. Moving the ark to another city only produced the same results. Many died and all were afflicted with the plague. In the end the Philistines, realizing that the plague was directly related to their possession of the ark, voluntarily returned the sacred chest to the Israelites. The Philistines were made to acknowledge the superiority of God, even though as polytheists they were unable to grasp the idea that there indeed was one god for all people.

Two important lessons about the nature of God can be learned here. One is that the defeat of the Israelites and the capture of the ark are not signs of God's weakness—these events instead demonstrate how God will, if necessary, use an outside force to discipline God's people. Second, the Philistines learned that God was stronger than their god, which in the end was nothing but a piece of clay smashed on the floor of his temple. Furthermore, they learned that God's power extends to all people, whether or not they choose to believe.

> The Philistines learned that God's power extends to all people, whether or not they choose to believe.

Dimension 3: What Does the Bible Mean to Us?

Quick Fixes to Life's Problems

Fear is a powerful motivator. When people are afraid, they sometimes make rash and even stupid decisions that can have serious repercussions for their lives and the life of their community. The elders of Israel did this when they decided to take the ark of the covenant into battle against the Philistines.

The Israelites had good reason to be afraid, as they had been attacked and soundly defeated. The reason for their defeat was their disobedience to God. But instead of seriously considering what they were doing that was wrong and how it could be corrected, the elders instead opted for what they hoped would be a "quick fix."

> We live in an age when people seek quick fixes to problems. But, as the Israelites learned, there are no easy, painless solutions to problems that result from sin and disobedience.

These spiritually bankrupt leaders believed that carrying the ark, the symbol of Almighty God, into battle would bring them victory. But as they learned, there are no easy, painless solutions to problems that result from sin and disobedience.

We too live in an age when people seek quick fixes to problems that need to be solved by serious analysis, sacrifice, and hard work. Today, many states and local governments are turning to legalized gambling to provide revenues to support such worthwhile projects as schools and senior citizen programs. Many politicians and their supporters see gambling revenues as quick fixes for programs that are starved for cash. They are afraid that the voters will not like it if services are cut or taxes are raised. But in the end, the long-term problems that gambling creates for individuals, families, and communities far outweigh its benefits.

We also see the "quick fix" approach to living in other areas of personal life. One-half of new marriages end in divorce because it is easier to split than to work together to iron out differences and to live up to one's wedding vows.

Like the Israelites, many people believe that even when we are disobedient, God will somehow work to bring us victory and happiness. But this is a mistaken assumption, for that is not the message

> In what area of your life are you tempted to seek a "quick fix"?

of the Bible. Surely God is ready and willing to forgive us when we stumble. God is always there to help us when we need the touch of a mighty hand. However, this does not mean that we can put God's name to whatever we are doing and expect the Lord to work on our behalf.

What the Israelites did with the ark might be likened to the modern practice of "wearing religion on our sleeve." The elders and keepers of the ark simply did not understand and respect their traditions. They did not know that the Lord God would not be manipulated by the whims of human beings. Likewise, those who casually use the name of God to justify whatever it is they want to do must recognize that this is sinful, even blasphemous behavior.

> **Are we people who use God's name to justify doing what we want to do?**

We must take seriously the biblical reality that people will be punished when they disobey God. God may even use nonbelievers like the Philistines to carry out that discipline on God's people. Using the name of God to legitimize what we are doing will not exempt us from the consequences of our actions.

As the Jews have learned throughout their long and difficult history, being "chosen" does not mean being selected for special privilege or being protected from the consequences of sin. Being covenant people means that we will be blessed, but it also means that we have added responsibilities and will be held to a higher moral standard than nonbelievers.

God Is on Our Side

In almost every war that is fought, people on both sides say that "God is on our side." Abraham Lincoln, president of the United States during our bloody Civil War, had a deep and abiding faith in God. He believed that he was an instrument in the hand of God in this war that was fought to save the Union and free the slaves.

However, unlike other leaders in that war, Lincoln did not hold the simplistic and arrogant belief that God was on his side. After the ruinous battle of Gettysburg in 1863, Lincoln began to believe that it was clear where God's judgment was coming down. The president believed that the judgment of God had fallen on the whole country, north and south. The United States was being punished for the sin of slavery. He believed that the nation must atone in blood for its complicity and wickedness in condoning slavery.

> **We need to be careful about how we use the name of God and Christ's church to legitimize what we want to do and what we would like to see happen.**

We need to be careful about how we use the name of God and Christ's church to legitimize what we want to do and what we would like to see happen. Rather than saying "God is on our side," we should listen to the words of Moses, who asked the covenant people, "Who is on the LORD's side?" (Exodus 32:26).

The God of All Peoples

The Philistines played an important part in the development of the covenant people. They tested the Israelites when they needed to be made stronger.

In this passage the Philistines are used as an instrument of God's punishment of the Hebrews. However, the Philistines themselves also learn an important lesson about God. They find that they too are subject to God's power and punishment. Human beings are never exempt from the presence and judgment of God, even though they may think they will not be held accountable.

The psalmist expressed it well—"Fools say in their hearts, 'There is no God' " (Psalm 14:1). This is as true today as it has ever been. Those who deny the reality and power of God over all people do so at their own peril. We do not need to look far to see people around us who are suffering because they refuse to believe in God or to take God seriously. This is a decision that every man and woman must make on his or her own. We all must answer the question, Who is God for me?

> Those who deny the reality and power of God over all people do so at their own peril. We all must answer the question, Who is God for me?

Dimension 4: A Daily Bible Journey Plan

Day 1: **1 Samuel 6:1-12**

Day 2: **1 Samuel 6:13-18**

Day 3: **1 Samuel 6:19–7:2**

Day 4: **1 Samuel 7:3-17**

Day 5: **1 Samuel 8**

Day 6: **1 Samuel 9:1-26**

Day 7: **1 Samuel 9:27–10:13**

3

1 Samuel 8

THE PEOPLE DEMAND A KING

What to Watch For

This lesson explains why the elders of Israel desired a king and Samuel's response to that request. Samuel dislikes the idea but decides to go along with it after he prays to God and receives the consent of God. Note that God comforts Samuel by assuring him that the people are not rejecting him personally and that his years of faithful service were not in vain. The real issue here is the failure of faith by the covenant people. The question is, Who is king of Israel?

Read 1 Samuel 8. Pay careful attention to the reasons why the elders want a king as well as Samuel's objections. They are concerned both about integrity in government and military security. The comment about wanting to be "like other nations" is revealing. Samuel's stern lecture on the demands that a king will place on the people fails to persuade the elders to withdraw their request.

Dimension 1:
What Does the Bible Say?

1. Why do the people feel the need to change their system of government? (1 Samuel 8:4-5, 19-20)

2. Why does the Lord tell Samuel to grant the wish of the elders? What does this tell us about God's relationship to the covenant people? (1 Samuel 8:7-9)

3. Make a list of the items that were considered to be the rights and privileges of a king. (1 Samuel 8:11-17)

Dimension 2: What Does the Bible Mean?

Samuel had served Israel well as judge, priest, prophet, and military leader. We read that under Samuel's leadership Israel subdued the Philistines and recovered the territory that this enemy had taken from them. "There was peace also between Israel and the Amorites" (1 Samuel 7:13-14).

As 1 Samuel 8 opens we see that Samuel has grown older. He is concerned about who will succeed him as leader of Israel. Quite understandably, Samuel hoped that his sons would fill his shoes. He therefore appoints his two sons, Joel and Abijah (uh-BIGH-juh), as judges in Beersheba, with the expectation that they would assume his leadership role.

However, Samuel's sons, like those of his mentor Eli, turned out to be men who lacked their father's faith in God and the personal integrity that is part and parcel of that faith. Joel and Abijah "took bribes and perverted justice" (1 Samuel 8:3). Unlike Eli, Samuel could not see and accept that his sons were unsuited to be judges of the covenant people.

Integrity in leadership has always been a major concern of Israelite religion and government. The greatest prophets in the Hebrew tradition forcefully condemned the corruption of their leaders.

Integrity in leadership has always been a major concern of Israelite religion and government. The law of Moses specifically condemned the taking of bribes. Exodus 23:8 warns, "You shall take no bribe, for a bribe blinds the officials, and subverts the cause of those who are in the right." The greatest prophets in the Hebrew tradition forcefully condemned the cor-

THE LORD'S RESTRICTIONS ON A KING
(Deuteronomy 17:15-20)

* No foreign kings
* Not too many horses
* Not too many wives
* Not too much gold and silver
* The law must remain with the king
* The king must observe and obey the law
* The king must not exalt himself above others

ruption of their leaders. Isaiah attacked those judges who "acquit the guilty for a bribe, and deprive the innocent of their rights" (Isaiah 5:23). Amos condemned those who "afflict the righteous, who take a bribe, and push aside the needy in the gate" (Amos 5:12).

Therefore one of the important reasons behind the elders' request for a king was this lack of confidence in Samuel's sons to lead the people with integrity and sound judgment. However, although the leaders were correct in questioning the fitness of Joel and Abijah to be their leaders, that alone did not justify the creation of a monarchy. The people were demanding a king for two other significant reasons.

> Philistia was the most formidable enemy that the Israelites had faced since claiming territory in Canaan. The Philistines had the most technically advanced military hardware, such as iron weapons and chariots.

When the Book of First Samuel opens, Israel is besieged by Philistine aggression. Philistia was the most formidable enemy that the Israelites had faced since claiming territory in Canaan. Under the leadership of various judges, the Israelites had fought successfully against other peoples such as the Moabites, the Midianites, and the Amorites. However, the Philistines were different. They had the most technically advanced military hardware, such as iron weapons and chariots. Their five city-states were well organized into a unified fighting force. (See map of Philistine territory on page 13.)

As we remember from the last chapter, even the ark of the covenant had been captured and removed to a Philistine city. The Israelites had lost territory to this powerful enemy, and some Israelite cities were paying tribute to the Philistines for protection. The Philistines posed the greatest threat to Israel's existence since their entry into the Promised Land.

Samuel had done a remarkably good job in beating back the Philistine threat, but now he was older and no longer an able warrior. The elders, who realized that his sons were unsuited to lead them, believed that their national security would be enhanced if the twelve tribes were united under a central government. Most of the other nations that surrounded Israel did have kings. These kings were often strong military leaders who were able to organize and inspire their people for battle. This is one reason why the elders wanted Israel to "be like other nations." The loose confederation of tribes that functioned under the leadership of the judges was limited in its fighting capabilities. The elders believed they were at a distinct disadvantage in times of war.

However, there was still another motivation behind the demand for a king. Throughout their early history, the Israelites were constantly tempted to worship the gods of the Canaanite peoples who surrounded them. They found the worship of these idols, which included sexual perversions, to be seductive. When they chased after these false gods, they were trying to be like these other people.

So it was also with their desire for a king. The Israelites envied their neighbors who possessed the glamour, glory, and power that surround a monarchy. They believed that if they could just "be like other nations," then they would be happy, because they would receive honor and respect from these other peoples.

> The Israelites believed that if they could just "be like other nations," then they would be happy, because they would receive honor and respect from these other peoples.

Samuel did not like this idea of a king at all. He must have been greatly disappointed that his sons would not succeed him as judges. He believed that the people were rejecting him personally—perhaps he felt that the people were being ungrateful to him for his many years of faithful service. God assured Samuel that this was not the case. God told Samuel that the people were not rejecting him but rather their God, which of course got at the real heart of the matter.

The decision to establish a monarchy was a significant turning point in Israel's history. Up until this time, the confederation of twelve tribes had been ruled fairly effectively by judges. We need to remember that these leaders were not judges with a strictly judicial vocation, as we understand judges today. These judges were not merely arbiters of disputes but rather charismatic personalities whom God raised up as leaders of the young nation. Deborah, Samson, Eli, and Samuel all governed the people with varying degrees of effectiveness. They can best be described as *deliverers*, men and women whom God chose to do specific work on behalf of the Lord. Some judges, for example Othniel, are portrayed as ideal leaders (Judges 3:7-11). On the other hand, Samson turned out to be a tragic figure because of his flawed character (Judges 14–16).

> The decision to establish a monarchy was a significant turning point in Israel's history. Until then, the confederation of twelve tribes had been ruled fairly effectively by judges.

At times Israel sinned and was given into the hands of its enemies for a specific period of time, such as the twenty years they spent under the hand of King Jabin of Canaan (Judges 4:1-3). When the people repented, God raised up a judge to set them free. However, the practice of worshiping idols (doing evil in the sight of the Lord) was continually repeated. This explains why the Israelites were in constant conflict with the peoples of Canaan and why Israel did not succeed in driving them out.

As the Philistine threat to the west grew stronger, it became clear to the elders that the present system of government was not providing adequate military security for Israel. If they had a king "like other nations," then they would be able to confront their enemies on equal ground, at least in terms of their military organization. Also, the reluctance of the elders to hand the reins of leadership over to Samuel's corrupt sons is understandable.

However, the most significant feature of government by judges was that there was no question that God was ruler and "king" of Israel. With the establishment of a monarchy, an unavoidable separation developed between the religious and secular life of Israel. Surely the kings should have realized that they ruled only by the grace and permission of God; but as Israel's history shows, the kings often forgot this first principle of governing the covenant people.

> **The most significant feature of government by judges was that there was no question that God was ruler and "king" of Israel.**

The end result of the decision to establish a monarchy was that Israel was no longer a *theocracy*, that is, a government ruled by God. With the change in political system, Israel lost some of the distinctiveness that God had intended for the Hebrews when they were chosen as the covenant people to serve as a "light to the nations" (Isaiah 42:6).

The desire for a king was, in fact, merely a symptom of Israel's sin in rejecting their God. Samuel raised thoughtful objections to the request. Indeed, his warnings were so on the mark that some scholars believe that Samuel's words were enhanced by editors from a later period who had seen firsthand what an autocratic king would demand of his people. These demands were exactly

> **The desire for a king was, in fact, merely a symptom of Israel's sin in rejecting their God.**

what Solomon required of the people during his opulent and powerful reign in the tenth century B.C.

Interestingly, Samuel did not speak of the "ways of the king" as being abuses. The taking of family members and crops and slaves for himself were simply the rights of a king. The one-tenth that would be exacted from the people would be in addition to the tenth that was to be given as a tithe to God.

In the end, Samuel was unable to persuade the people to change their minds. God told Samuel to give in to their wishes. Note that there was never any question that God would be the one to select the king, who would be anointed by God's faithful servant Samuel.

Correct Diagnosis—Wrong Treatment

One of the amazing aspects about living in the late twentieth century is how quickly technologies change. For example, computers and programs that were "revolutionary" just a few years ago are now outdated. It seems like every week we hear of some new information or communication revolution that will radically change people's lives.

Paul Saffo, a director at the Institute for the Future, argues that "historic advances in technology are invariably accompanied by a cycle of hyperbole followed by disillusionment.

" 'It's a consistent pattern in our response to new technologies,' he remarked. 'We simultaneously overestimate the short-term impact and underestimate its long-term impact.' " (From "Changing the Wiring Takes Time," *New York Times*, October 30, 1994, section 4, pages 1, 4.)

This statement could well describe what happened to the people of Israel as they made their transition from a confederacy of tribes to a monarchy. As we have said, the elders had legitimate reasons for wanting a change in their governmental structure. They could see better than Samuel that his sons were not suited to lead God's people. They also realized that the Israelites were at a disadvantage when they went into battle against enemies who were unified under the leadership of a king.

> Judges 21:25 gives a final verdict on the leadership of the judges: this loose system of authority was not successful in helping the people maintain high standards of faith and morality.

We need also to remember the closing words of the Book of Judges: "In those days there was no king in Israel; all the people did what was right in their own eyes." These words imply that the final verdict on the leadership of the judges was that this loose system of authority was not successful in helping the people maintain high standards of faith and morality. The covenant demanded, not that people do what was "right in their own eyes," but rather do what was right in God's eyes.

Therefore the elders of Israel made the correct diagnosis when they concluded that it was time for a change, even though their judge Samuel had provided them with outstanding leadership characterized by a high level of moral integrity. The elders believed that they would not see the likes of Samuel again.

However, as is so often the case, the correct diagnosis did not necessarily lead to the right treatment. Overall, the history of Israel's monarchy is a sad story of corruption and apostasy. Samuel's prophetic words concerning the ways of the king came true. Even worse than the burdens that the kings laid on their people was the way in which so many of them chased after the idols of their pagan neighbors.

Is Change Always for the Better?

An old proverb says, "Be careful what you ask for—you may get it." This wise saying aptly describes what happened to the people of Israel. Their "dream come true" proved, in the end, to be their undoing. Under Solomon's glorious reign they were heavily taxed and overworked. Finally they were forced into exile as God's punishment for sins that were largely the responsibility of their wicked kings. They never fully recovered from that experience.

We want change, but we want it on our own terms.

We too desperately want our dreams to come true. But the problem is that the changes we want to make in our lives may not be what God wants for us. We want change, but we want it on our own terms. That which we think will bring us joy so often brings unhappiness and despair.

Again, reflecting on the advances in technology in modern society, we too realize that change does not always make things better. Despite more powerful computers, car phones, cable television, and better designed automobiles, life does not really feel that much different for most people. They still have many of the same relational problems with spouses, parents, children, and coworkers that people have always had. The key question is: Have all of these changes really made people any happier?

The children of Israel believed that if they could only have a king and "be like other nations," then they too could have security, prosperity, power, and prestige. But as the sad history of Israel's kings demonstrates, it did not work out that way. The kings did not bring the Israelites peace and happiness, only pain and despair.

We have a cartoon on the door of our refrigerator. It shows a little girl standing in front of the tree on Christmas morning surrounded by piles of new toys. The caption reads, "Mommy I'm bored."

So often we are like that little girl. We think that a new car, a larger salary, or a bigger home in an up-and-coming location will make us happier. An economist recently reported that most Americans, no matter what their level of income, believe that if they could earn 25 percent more money than they make now, then they would be happy. This is true for people from all socio-economic levels. However, when people achieve that one-fourth increase, they desire another 25 percent increase. The increased income is not saved and invested but instead fuels increased spending.

It almost never happens that people who are able to achieve the "bigger and better" changes in their lives find true happiness. The reason is that these kinds of changes do not usually contribute to our spiritual well-being.

The Israelite demand for a king was flawed in another sense. It is true, as the elders correctly ascertained, that a community needs strong and faithful leadership to accomplish almost anything worthwhile. There is no substitute for enlightened leadership that provides goals and direction for people. When people go their own way and "do their own thing," the result is often chaos, inertia, and decadence.

> Making "bigger and better" changes in our lives does not bring true happiness. The reason is that these kinds of changes do not usually contribute to our spiritual well-being.

However, the real danger lies in the thirst for leadership. We look to our leaders to provide us with security and prosperity. But the problem is that sometimes we think that turning responsibility over to a leader frees us from the personal responsibility to take care of ourselves and our loved ones. This was the mistake that the Israelites made when they opted for kings who turned out to be autocratic rulers who led them astray from their God.

The American democracy is truly a brilliant form of government. We have elected leaders who are always accountable to the people. This system has allowed the United States to become a great country among the nations of the world.

Often there is much dissatisfaction with our elected officials, however. Certainly they may have their shortcomings, but the lack of leadership that we decry is also the fault of the people who are governed. Do we expect too much of our leaders? Have we tried to turn too much responsibility for our lives over to the politicians? And most importantly, do people really understand that in order for there to be effective leadership, there must be men and women who are willing to be enlightened and responsible followers?

> We cannot expect to be governed responsibly when we do not make any effort to be enlightened and responsible citizens.

A post-election political cartoon shows a man blurting out to his friends, "Don't blame me; I didn't vote." We cannot expect to be governed responsibly when we do not make any effort to be enlightened and responsible citizens. We must remember that God is our king, that we and our leaders serve here only by the grace of God.

Dimension 4:
A Daily Bible Journey Plan

Day 1: 1 Samuel 10:14-27

Day 2: 1 Samuel 11

Day 3: 1 Samuel 12

Day 4: 1 Samuel 13:1-15b

Day 5: 1 Samuel 13:15c-22

Day 6: 1 Samuel 13:23–14:23

Day 7: 1 Samuel 14:24-35

1 Samuel 10:17-24; 13:1-15

4

ISRAEL'S FIRST KING: SAUL, WHO HID HIMSELF AMONG THE BAGGAGE

What to Watch For

This lesson will look at two passages in First Samuel. The first, 1 Samuel 10:17-24, tells of Saul's confirmation as king of Israel. The second, 1 Samuel 13:1-15, reports the circumstances surrounding the beginning of the end of Saul's reign.

● 1 Samuel 10:17-24. The people demand a king. Lots are cast and Saul is confirmed as king. But when the time comes for Saul to be heralded as king, he is nowhere to be found. He is hiding "among the baggage." Saul is brought before the people; and the people proclaim, "Long live the king!"

● 1 Samuel 13:1-15. Saul finds himself at war with the Philistines. After deploying his troops, Saul awaits Samuel's arrival to offer sacrifice before battle. But Samuel's arrival is delayed. So Saul offers the sacrifice himself. When Samuel arrives, he declares that, because Saul took upon himself responsibilities reserved for religious functionaries, Saul's kingship is going to collapse.

1. What differing attitudes toward kingship are expressed in 1 Samuel 10:17-24?

2. What did the Israelites do when they saw the mighty Philistine army and "were in distress"? (1 Samuel 13:5-7)

3. What did Saul do when Samuel did not arrive at the appointed time? (1 Samuel 13:8-9)

4. How did Saul explain his actions to Samuel? What was Samuel's response? (1 Samuel 13:11-14)

SETTING THE STAGE

The previous chapter looked at 1 Samuel 8, which records Israel's demand for a king and God's response to this request (1 Samuel 8:4-9, 19-22). First Samuel 9:1–10:8 tells the story of how Samuel met Saul, son of Kish, and anointed him in a private ceremony to be the first king of Israel. In the first passage in this lesson, Saul is confirmed as king in a public ceremony.

1 Samuel 10:17-24

As this passage opens, Samuel has "summoned the people to the LORD at Mizpah" (10:17), the gathering place for the people of Israel at this time (see also Judges 20–21). Mizpah, Bethel, and Gilgal were three locations where Samuel "judged Israel all the days of his life" (1 Samuel 7:15-16).

In 1 Samuel 10:18-19, Samuel utters an oracle in which he summarizes the debate that had occurred in 1 Samuel 8 between the people and God about whether Israel should have a human king. He reminds the people of Israel about what the power of God had done for them and how they had "rejected" the divine king and insisted on having a human king set over them. So, reluctantly, Samuel had agreed to set a king over the people.

To identify the individual who would be the first king of Israel, Samuel casts lots (10:20-21).

Playing the Lottery

It may seem strange to the modern reader of 1 Samuel 10:17-24 that Saul's confirmation as king came through a lottery. Chances are, when we think of lotteries, we think of a state lottery and a chance to win millions of dollars. But in the biblical world, a lottery was viewed as a way for God to communicate the divine will to humans. Proverbs 16:33 affirms that when the lot is cast, "the decision is the LORD's alone."

> In the biblical world, a lottery was viewed as a way for God to communicate the divine will to humans.

We do not know exactly how the lot was taken in the world of the Bible. Presumably, stones, pieces of clay, or other objects, perhaps inscribed with letters or symbols, were placed in a vessel. Then, the vessel was shaken until one of the objects flew out. Or, perhaps someone drew one of the objects out of the vessel.

The Bible records several occasions on which lots were cast in order to determine the divine will and/or carry out the functions of the community of the people of God. (See for example, Leviticus 16:7-10; Numbers 26:55; Joshua 14:2; 1 Samuel 14:42; and Acts 1:26.) So, it is quite in keeping with biblical tradition that Saul was confirmed as king of Israel through the casting of lots.

But notice 1 Samuel 10:21c: When the lottery identified Saul son of Kish as the person who would be Israel's first king, he was nowhere to be found. In 1 Samuel 9:21, Saul expresses serious doubts about his own qualifications to be the one "on whom is all Israel's desire fixed" (9:20). Now, on the occasion of his confirmation as king of Israel, he tries to hide to avoid the leadership role that is being thrust upon him. Saul, the reluctant king, on what we would call his inauguration day, has "hidden himself among the baggage" (10:22).

Eventually, Saul was found, brought before the people, and heralded as king (10:23-24).

Between the first passage in this lesson, 1 Samuel 10:17-24, and the second, 1 Samuel 13:1-15, Saul begins his reign on a positive note. In 1 Samuel 10:27–11:15, Saul wins an important victory against the Ammonites. Then, in 1 Samuel 12, perhaps in response to Saul's victory against the Ammonites, the aging Samuel formally relinquishes to the king responsibility for the leadership of Israel.

1 Samuel 13:1-15

The numbers in the opening verse of 1 Samuel 13 are not clear in the Hebrew text. We are not sure how old Saul was when he began to reign. Nor are we sure how long he reigned over Israel.

In verses 2 through 4 of 1 Samuel 13, Saul deploys his troops against the Philistines. Jonathan makes the first strike against the Philistines and defeats the Philistine garrison stationed at Geba. This reckless attack begins all-out war. And, with war looming on the horizon, "the people were called out to join Saul at Gilgal."

Verses 5-7 describe the desperate situation in which Saul and the Israelites found themselves when confronted with the might of the massive Philistine army. Assembled for battle against Israel were "thirty thousand chariots, and six thousand horsemen." The chariots and mounted combat personnel were completely impractical in the hill country of Palestine. A more serious threat to the Israelites was the Philistine infantry, described by the narrator as being "like the sand on the seashore in multitude."

Fear struck the hearts of the Israelites at the sight of the vast Philistine army. Some of the Israelites, we are told, escaped and hid in the caves and crevices that can be found throughout the hill country of Palestine. Others decided to leave Palestine entirely. These fled as refugees of war across the Jordan River into the regions of Gad and Gilead on the eastern side of the Jordan. For upwards of two hundred years, since the time of Joshua, the Hebrews had been trying to secure their presence in Canaan. But now, the settlement in the Promised Land was beginning to reverse. The advances made in the land by Joshua and the judges were breaking down. Some of the Israelites were beginning to retreat out of Canaan back to the eastern side of the Jordan River. By fleeing from the Promised Land in fear, the Israelites were putting in jeopardy the fulfillment of God's promises.

The future of Israel was at stake. Saul had to do something. The king who did not really want to be

> The future of Israel was at stake. Saul, the king who did not really want to be king, was going to have to act like a king

king was going to have to act like a king whether he wanted to or not. He could hide from responsibility no longer.

This is the context for the incident in 1 Samuel 13:8-14. The events recorded in these verses presuppose the instructions that Samuel had given to Saul in 10:8. Samuel had told Saul to "go down to Gilgal ahead of me; then I will come down to you to present burnt offerings and offer sacrifices of well-being. Seven days you shall wait, until I come to you and show you what you shall do."

Saul followed Samuel's instructions. He went to Gilgal and waited for seven days. As noted at the beginning of our discussion of 1 Samuel 10:17-24, Gilgal was one of three locations where Samuel "judged Israel" (1 Samuel 7:16). Apparently, Samuel was intending to finish his ministry at one of the other two sites, then move on to Gilgal to begin his ministry there. When he arrived at Gilgal, one of the first services he would perform would be to offer sacrifice to God on behalf of Saul and the Israelite army.

But Samuel did not arrive after seven days. No explanation is given for his failure to arrive on time. As Saul waited and waited for Samuel to arrive at Gilgal, his ill-trained troops, already suffering from fear and low morale, began to "slip away" (13:8). And so, in Samuel's absence, Saul offered the sacrifices himself. As the king of Israel, Saul could rule over the people and lead the army into war. He was not, however, supposed to serve as priest and offer sacrifice to God.

No sooner had Saul finished offering the sacrifices to God than Samuel arrived. Greatly disturbed by Saul's actions, Samuel declared that Saul had acted "foolishly" and had "not kept the commandment of the LORD your God." Then, in a declaration that shaped the history of Israel for the next four hundred years and paved the way for the emergence of a messiah from the Davidic line, Samuel announced that, because of Saul's presumptuous behavior, his kingdom would not last. His descendants would not inherit his throne. Rather, Samuel told Saul, God had chosen someone else to become ruler over Israel.

Dimension 3:
What Does the Bible Mean to Us?

The two Scripture passages we are looking at in this lesson prompt us to think about reluctance to accept leadership roles and the sometimes difficult realities of leadership. Indeed, I suspect that the realities of leadership, such as we see in our second Scripture passage, frequently cause people, like Saul in our first passage, to be reluctant to accept new leadership roles.

Accepting Leadership Roles

The church that I serve has just finished the annual process of filling the slate of officers for the coming year. Every year some of the people who are invited to accept leadership roles decline the invitation. Many have good reasons—responsibilities at work, family responsibilities, recuperation from a recent medical problem, and so on. Other people, though, like Saul in 1 Samuel 9:21, express feelings of inadequacy. They do not think that they are up to the task, that they are good enough, that they are worthy. Few people go so far as to hide, like Saul in 1 Samuel 10:22, when invited to serve on a church board or committee. But I suspect that many would like to.

I have served for six years on the annual conference board that interviews candidates for ordained ministry. As I have interviewed women and men seeking ordination, I have frequently seen hesitancy and reluctance to accept God's call to service. Some candidates have shared with our board that they have been running from God's call to ministry for years, trying, like Saul, to hide among the clutter and "baggage" of life. They have expressed a deep concern that they would be unable to fulfill the responsibilities of ordained ministry. Some candidates also believe that they are unworthy of the calling.

> Some of us have been running from God's call to ministry for years, trying, like Saul, to hide among the clutter and "baggage" of life.

Most of us, at one time or another, have felt reluctance to accept leadership positions in the church. We may feel overwhelmed by the task that we are asked to perform. Sometimes, like Saul, rather than accepting responsibility for leadership, we would prefer to go off by ourselves and hide.

Saul was in good biblical company when he showed reluctance to accept responsibility and so are we when we balk at the idea of saying yes to something that we have been asked to do. Moses (Exodus 3:11; 4:10, 13), Gideon (Judges 6:15), and Jeremiah (Jeremiah 1:6) all expressed reluctance to accept the responsibility of their call from God. But to each of these three great leaders God offered a wonderful promise. God promised Moses, Gideon, and Jeremiah, "I will be/am with you" (Exodus 3:12; Judges 6:16; Jeremiah 1:8). It is comforting for us to know that when God calls us to positions of responsibility, God stays with us to help us fulfill our calling.

The Difficult Realities of Accepting Responsibility

Once we do accept responsibility for a position of leadership, life is not always easy. Saul found himself in a "Catch 22." There was no easy solution to his dilemma. Unfortunately, the realities of accepting responsibility are such that making difficult decisions is a part of being a leader. The story of Saul's dilemma suggests several things about making difficult decisions.

First, Saul's story cautions us against making decisions out of fear. Fear can push us to make ill-conceived decisions and hasty decisions.

Second, the story of Saul's dilemma cautions us against impatience. A parishioner recently reminded me of the joke about the person who

> 1. Do not make decisions out of fear.
> 2. Impatience can ruin the best planned progress.
> 3. Good intentions are not enough.

prayed, "O God, give me patience. And give it to me *NOW!*" We do not like to be patient. Yet impatience can ruin even the best planned progress. From candymaking, to planting a garden, to speaking with someone about a delicate matter, if the action is not carried out at just the right time, the plan might be ruined. We ought not to allow impatience to be the motivating factor in our actions.

Third, we learn from the story of Saul that, sometimes, good intentions are not enough. When I taught this passage not long ago, one of my students reminded me of the old declaration that, "The road to destruction is paved with good intentions." Saul, indeed, had good intentions (verses 11-12). But his good intentions did not guarantee that his decision was the correct one. Churches and organizations frequently begin new ventures with good intentions. But programs that *seem* wonderful sometimes end up doing a great deal of damage.

When faced with a difficult decision, a good decision-making process can be helpful. A few years ago my wife and I led the youth of our church in a workshop on how to make difficult decisions. Using a series of video-tapes, Joy and I outlined for our teens a six-step process in decision-making. The six steps are as follows:

1. Know your values.
2. Set goals.
3. Expand your alternatives.
4. Seek (critical) information.
5. Predict outcomes.
6. Take action.

I wonder what Saul would have done in his dilemma if he had followed this six-step process in decision-making.

Day 1: 1 Samuel 14:36-48

Day 2: 1 Samuel 14:49–15:9

Day 3: 1 Samuel 15:10-35

Day 4: 1 Samuel 16:1-13

Day 5: 1 Samuel 16:14-23

Day 6: 1 Samuel 17:1-30

Day 7: 1 Samuel 17:31-58

1 Samuel 16:1-13; 17:41–18:9

5

*F*AITH THE SIZE OF SLING STONES

What to Watch For

This chapter examines two excerpts from the early part of the story of David: 1 Samuel 16:1-13 and 1 Samuel 17:41–18:9.

● 1 Samuel 16:1-13. These verses give the account of David's anointing by Samuel as the second king of Israel. As you study this passage, watch particularly for insights into how *humans* tend to look at people versus how *God* looks at people. Watch also for the description of what happened to David when he was anointed.

● 1 Samuel 17:41–18:9. This passage is the conclusion of the famous story of David's victory over the Philistine giant Goliath. You may want to read all of 1 Samuel 17:1–18:16. As you study this passage, watch for David's affirmation of how the people of God achieve victory over gigantic problems in life. Watch also for David's declaration of how victories are *not* achieved.

Dimension 1:
What Does the Bible Say?

1. What happens to David when Samuel anoints him? (1 Samuel 16:13)

37

2. According to 1 Samuel 16, how do humans tend to judge people? How does God look at people? (1 Samuel 16:6-7)

3. Goliath came to David "with sword and spear and javelin." How does David say he presents himself before Goliath? (1 Samuel 17:45)

4. What common weapons does 1 Samuel 17 say God does *not* use in order to save? (1 Samuel 17:46-47)

Dimension 2: What Does the Bible Mean?

SETTING THE STAGE

Near the end of the second Scripture passage studied in the previous lesson, Samuel declares that Saul's rule over Israel is going to end and that God has selected someone else to serve as king (1 Samuel 13:13-14). That person who would be Saul's replacement on the throne is identified in the first passage to be studied in this lesson.

1 Samuel 16:1-13

In 1 Samuel 16:1, God sends Samuel to find "Jesse the Bethlehemite" and to anoint one of Jesse's sons as the next king of Israel. But Saul was still king of Israel, and any attempt by Samuel to anoint a new king would almost certainly be construed by Saul as an act of treason (16:2). So God told Samuel to go to Bethlehem and to anoint the next king in a private ceremony as part of a worship service to which Jesse and his family were to be invited (16:2-3).

Samuel followed God's command and went to Bethlehem to begin the ritual (16:4). The sons of Jesse marched before Samuel, while Samuel waited to anoint the chosen one of God as the next king of Israel. Eliab (i-LIGH-uhb), Jesse's first son, impressed Samuel (16:6). God, however, was not impressed (16:7). God does not, as we would say, "judge a book by its cover." "The LORD does not see as mortals see; they look on the outward appearance, but the LORD looks on the heart." God challenged Samuel not to use outward appearance as the determining factor in judging leadership qualities.

One by one the sons of Jesse passed before Samuel. And one by one God rejected them. Finally David, the youngest son of Jesse, was brought in from the pasture where he had been tending the sheep (16:11-12). When David passed before Samuel, God instructed the prophet, "Rise and anoint him; for this is the one" (16:12c). So

> "The LORD does not see as mortals see; they look on the outward appearance, but the LORD looks on the heart."

Samuel anointed the young shepherd, "and the spirit of the LORD came mightily upon David from that day forward" (16:13).

The anointing of a king was a ritual similar to our sacrament of baptism. Only, instead of placing water on a person's head, Samuel placed a sweet-smelling oil on the head of the person who would be king. The sweet-smelling oil used for anointing was made from a recipe provided in Exodus 30:22-25. Just as baptism is an outward and visible symbol of something that God is doing spiritually in a person's life, so the anointing of the new king of Israel was an outward and visible symbol of something that God was doing in the new king's life. Indeed, in 1 Samuel 16:13, when the outward and visible action of anointing takes place, the spirit of God empowers David.

Some of David's brothers may, by human standards, have been just as well-qualified for kingship as David, maybe even more qualified. David was but a shepherd. He was the youngest of the sons of Jesse. But he was God's chosen, God's anointed. "The spirit of the LORD" had come "mightily upon" him. Once the Spirit "came mightily upon" him, David was able to do mighty things, giant-sized things.

MEANWHILE...

As 1 Samuel 17 opens, the Philistines and the Israelites have faced off in the Valley of Elah (EE-luh; the name means the Valley of the Great Tree). The Valley of Elah is a lovely, fertile, well-watered streambed valley fourteen or fifteen miles west/southwest of Bethlehem.

● Verses 4 through 11 of 1 Samuel 17 introduce the reader to the Philistine warrior Goliath from the city of Gath. Gath was one of the five Philistine city-states. The other four Philistine cities were Gaza, Ashkelon,

Ashdod, and Ekron. (See map on page 13.) Some ancient manuscripts report in verse 4 that Goliath was "six cubits and a span" tall. Other ancient manuscripts report in verse 4 that Goliath's height was "four cubits and a span." A cubit was equal to eighteen inches, a span about nine inches. So, according to some manuscripts, Goliath was nine feet, nine inches tall; in other manuscripts, he is described as being six feet, nine inches tall.

• Verses 12-40 introduce David in the story and report the circumstances of his arrival on the battlefield, his offer to fight the Philistine warrior, and his preparations for battle. The section concludes in verse 40 with the report that David "chose five smooth stones from the wadi [*wadi* is the Arabic word for a streambed], and put them in his shepherd's bag, in the pouch; his sling was in his hand, and he drew near to the Philistine."

Display of sling and stones from James L. Kelso Bible Lands Museum, Pittsburgh Theological Seminary. The caption in part says, "sling stones such as that which slew Goliath are found in quantity and . . . were thrown with such force that often they split in half."

SLINGING STONES

The ancient Near Eastern sling was not the kind of slingshot that we think of here in the United States. The sling that David used and the type of sling that youths still use in the Near East is made of a small pouch attached to the middle of a long leather thong or rope. The user places a stone in the pouch then brings the two ends of the thong or rope together, thereby closing the pouch. With both ends of the rope in hand, the pouch is swung over the head until great momentum is achieved. Then with the sling still rotating overhead, at precisely the right moment, the user releases one end of the thong, thereby opening the pouch and sending the stone hurling toward its target.

The stones that are used in Near Eastern slings are not the small pebble-type stones that we might expect. They are golfball to baseball size stones that, when hurled from a sling with great force, can cause serious injury.

Occasionally, if you are watching a news story from the Near East on television, you can still see Palestinian boys using slings in much the same way as David did on the battlefield in the Valley of Elah. I remember watching one news story in particular some years ago on CNN that brought the David and Goliath story to life for me. The Palestinian Intifada against Israeli occupation of the West Bank had been going on for about a year. Clashes between Israeli security forces and Palestinians who lived in the villages and towns of the West Bank were becoming more numerous and more violent. In CNN footage of one of these clashes a young Palestinian boy could be seen in the front of the foray wielding a sling over his head, preparing to release his stone with awesome accuracy and tremendous force against the Israeli troops who were threatening his village. Just as in biblical times, here was a youth, armed with but a sling and a stone, who had the courage and resolve to face head-on a powerful foe who threatened his people.

1 Samuel 17:41–18:9

Some years ago, I visited the Valley of Elah. Like David, I reached to the ground and picked up five stones. I thought how, centuries ago, in the valley where I stood, two armies clashed, and how a youth named David had faced a great warrior who was far better armed and more experienced than he. I looked at the stones in my hand, and I thought about the ways in which the power of God can work in and through the lives of even the most unlikely people.

In 1 Samuel 17:41-51a, Goliath and David meet on the battlefield. The dialogue between Goliath and David that precedes the battle (17:41-47) is actually more significant than the brief account of the battle itself. In the dialogue between Goliath and David can be found the religious message of the story of David's victory over Goliath—the message that, if God's people have even a little faith, God will bring them victory over their problems, even gigantic ones.

> The message of the David and Goliath story is that, if God's people have even a little faith, God will bring them victory over their problems, even gigantic ones.

The wording of 1 Samuel 17:42 recalls 16:12, the description of David when he was anointed by Samuel as the next king of Israel. While in 1 Samuel 16:12, the narrator describes David as "ruddy" and "handsome" as a way of praising David, in Goliath's eyes these qualities were cause for "disdain." Goliath's "disdain" is expressed in the giant's scornful comments to David in verses 43-44. Not only is David "only a youth, ruddy and handsome in appearance," but, as Goliath points out, he does not come into battle with conventional weapons (17:43). Goliath curses David in the names of the Philistine deities (17:43b) and threatens David (17:44).

In reply, David utters an affirmation that begins to focus on the message of the story (17:45). David declares that, while Goliath relies on conventional weaponry made by human hands, David comes against the giant armed with "the name of the LORD of hosts." David puts his trust in God, not human weaponry and power. David concludes his prebattle confession of faith by declaring that "the battle is the LORD's" and that God will bring victory to the people of God in order that "all this assembly may know that the LORD does not save by sword and spear . . . and he will give you [Goliath] into our hand" (17:47).

> Might, power, force, and human ingenuity do not help us overcome our problems in life. Rather, the people of God achieve victory through faithful reliance on the power of God.

Verses 41-47 of 1 Samuel 17 proclaim the message of the story of David and Goliath with striking clarity: It is not through might, power, force, and human ingenuity that the people of God overcome their problems in life. Rather, it is through faithful reliance on the power of God to save that the people of God achieve victory over their burdens, trials, and tribulations.

The narrator of the story of David and Goliath is astonishingly brief in the report of the actual battle. The text records in great detail the preparations for the battle and the prebattle dialogue between the combatants. But when the battle actually takes place, it is reported in only three and a half verses (17:48-51c). The way the narrator tells the story, we get the feeling that the battle was over before anyone knew what was happening.

David shot a stone from his sling, and it knocked the giant to the ground. Thus "David prevailed over the Philistine," not with the usual weapons of war, but through the power of God, "with a sling and a stone" (17:50). The text emphasizes that "there was no sword in David's hand." The account of the battle concludes with David using Goliath's own sword to cut off Goliath's head as a trophy.

Verses 51d-54 of 1 Samuel 17 report the complete rout of the Philistines by the Israelite army. The Israelites, encouraged by David's victory over Goliath, charge the enemy and force the Philistines to retreat all the way back to Philistia, to the two city-states of Gath and Ekron (verses 51d-52).

After the battle, Saul inquired about the identity of the young combatant who brought victory to the people of God. David introduces himself to King Saul in the last verse of 1 Samuel 17: "I am the son of your servant Jesse the Bethlehemite."

In verses 1-4 of 1 Samuel 18, David makes a new friend—Jonathan, son of Saul. "The soul of Jonathan," we read in 1 Samuel 18:1, "was bound to the soul of David." The depth of the new friendship becomes evident in 18:3 where it is reported that "Jonathan made a covenant with David, because he loved him as his own soul." Jonathan's actions in verse 4 are significant. It would seem that, by giving David "the robe that he was wearing, . . . and his armor, and even his sword and his bow and his belt," Jonathan was relinquishing his claim to the throne of Israel. Somehow, Jonathan, the crown prince, seemed to have realized that he was not going to succeed his father on the throne. Rather, David was going to be the next king.

Verse 2 of 1 Samuel 18 reports that Saul took David with him and would not let him return to his father's house. Saul apparently was greatly impressed by David and initially took a liking to him. How quickly things can change, though.

> Somehow, Jonathan, the crown prince, seemed to have realized that he was not going to succeed his father on the throne. Rather, David was going to be the next king.

The concluding verses of the second primary text for this chapter, 1 Samuel 18:5-9, show us a David who "was successful" in all that he did and was rewarded by King Saul with a command position in the army of Israel. These verses, though, also show us a king who began to feel envy toward David (this theme will be examined in detail in the next chapter). When the people of Israel were welcoming the victorious Israelite army home from the war against the Philistines, the women sang a song that praised Saul: "Saul has killed his thousands." But the song praised David even more: "David [has killed] his ten thousands" (18:7). That the people were giving such praise to David was more than Saul could stand. The king correctly saw in David great leadership potential; and he wondered, "What more can he have but the

43

kingdom?" (18:8c). The primary text for this lesson concludes with the ominous observation that "Saul eyed David from that day on," meaning that Saul's heart burned with envy against David from then on.

The account of David's victory over Goliath is a classic story of an underdog who ends up on top. We enjoy stories of small, weak, powerless forces rising up and vanquishing superpowers. Whether it is a story of a consumer who wins a battle against a giant, multinational corporation or an underdog athletic team upsetting a major powerhouse, we like to see the little guy win. The story of David slaying the Philistine giant Goliath is inspiring and gives us hope as we face such giant-size obstacles in our lives.

We see in the story of David and Goliath the power of faith. People just like you and me, if we have faith in God, if we have faith even the size of a sling stone, or as Jesus put it, if we have faith even the size of a mustard seed (Matthew 17:20), can face head-on the difficulties and obstacles in our lives that seem gigantic and be victorious over them.

> We can face the personal giants in life knowing that God is with us to grant us courage, wisdom, strength, and power.

We all occasionally face giants in life, personal giants that can cause us and our families severe distress and deep emotional turmoil. We face gigantic obstacles in life that can weaken our faith and shake our courage. But, like David, we can face these gigantic obstacles in life with a powerful ally. We can face the personal giants in life knowing that God is with us to grant us courage, wisdom, strength, and power. What are the personal giants that confront you?

For some of us, a personal giant may be a decision we have to make. We may be facing a decision having to do with our job or our family. The decision facing us may be complex and difficult. We are confused. No option seems appropriate. We lie awake at night distressed by the enormity of the problem. For us, the problem needing a decision seems like Goliath; and we feel like David, trying to make our decision with but a sling and a stone.

For others, a gigantic problem may be family oriented. Sometimes we face difficulties with children, parents, brothers, or sisters, problems that seem enormous. Sometimes we face broken relationships and shattered hopes and dreams. Such crises can tear us and our families apart. When there is a Goliath-size difficulty in the home among those whom we love, we may feel like David facing the problem with only a sling and a stone.

When, within the family, there is conflict, turmoil, anguish, and an absence of love, the problem often seems colossal and the solution far away.

For still others, a Goliath-sized problem may be substance abuse. Alcoholism and other drug abuse appear as powerful giants threatening our welfare and the happiness and security of home life.

Our gigantic problems may also be economic. Giant-sized stacks of bills, unexpected debts, and un- or underemployment can strain family relationships and home life. Or, a Goliath in life that must be faced with courage and strength may be sickness.

> Not all the giants that need to be vanquished are personal. We are often confronted with community problems that seem like Goliaths.

Not all the giants that need to be vanquished are personal. Goliath threatened, not just David, but the people of Israel as a whole. Frequently, we are confronted with community problems that seem like Goliaths— crime in the streets, health care, homelessness, un- or underemployment, domestic violence. Some of these gigantic problems may affect us personally. Others may not. But all these giant-sized problems are Goliaths that need to be vanquished nonetheless.

At least two observations can be made on how we can face personal and community giants head-on and be victorious over them. The first observation is that our battles in life are not won by might or personal power. Giant-sized problems in life are not solved by force. The narrative of the story of David and Goliath goes to great pains to emphasize this. David rejected Saul's armor and weaponry as the means by which Goliath would be vanquished. And David made this point quite clear in his challenge to Goliath in 1 Samuel 17:45-47.

The second observation on how we can be victorious over our personal and community Goliaths focuses on faith. The story of David and Goliath suggests to us that, if we have faith in God, even faith the size of a sling and a stone, when we confront our problems in life head-on, we will emerge victorious. We can face our personal Goliaths confident that God will help us vanquish our problems and slay personal and community giants that threaten our happiness and welfare. With God's help, and with faith moving us forward, there is no limit to what we can do. Ultimately, it is the power of God that gives us the victory and not we ourselves.

> Our battles in life are not won by might or personal power. If we have faith in God, even faith the size of a sling and a stone, when we confront our problems in life head-on, we will emerge victorious.

What is your personal giant that needs to be slain? Loneliness? Grief? Sickness? Inner-turmoil? Depression? Family problems? Substance abuse?

What giant is threatening your community? Crime? Economic problems? Domestic abuse? Pick up your stones and sling of faith in God and march forward in life confident that God is with you, confident that God will never let you down. Face your problem head-on, knowing that ultimately God will give you the strength to vanquish your personal and community Goliath.

Dimension 4:
A Daily Bible Journey Plan

Day 1: 1 Samuel 18:1-16

Day 2: 1 Samuel 18:17-30

Day 3: 1 Samuel 19

Day 4: 1 Samuel 20:1-23

Day 5: 1 Samuel 20:24-42

Day 6: 1 Samuel 21

Day 7: 1 Samuel 22

1 Samuel 19:1-17

DAVID FLEES FROM SAUL

What to Watch For

This lesson examines 1 Samuel 19:1-17. This passage can be divided into two sections: verses 1-7 and verses 8-17.

● 1 Samuel 19:1-7. As Saul's jealousy of David's success and fame burns hotter and hotter, the day comes when Saul decides to try to kill David. But Jonathan, Saul's son, intercedes on David's behalf. And Saul, at least for now, turns from his plot to kill David.

● 1 Samuel 19:8-17. Quickly forgetting his oath that he would not try to kill David (19:6), Saul twice makes attempts on David's life. He first tries to kill him with a spear. But David escapes. When that attempt on David's life fails, Saul sends assassins to David's home to try to kill him there. But with the help of his wife, Michal (MIGH-kuhl), David escapes again.

Dimension 1:
What Does the Bible Say?

1. At the beginning of 1 Samuel 19, Saul and Jonathan discuss David. Summarize their discussion in your own words.

2. How does Saul first try to kill David? (1 Samuel 19:10)

3. What two things does David's wife Michal do to help her husband escape from Saul a second time? (1 Samuel 19:12-13)

Dimension 2:
What Does the Bible Mean?

SETTING THE STAGE

At the end of the passage studied in the preceding lesson, David returns home with the Israelite army to the cheers of the people. David is welcomed as a hero for his military prowess against the Philistine giant Goliath (1 Samuel 18:6-7). Saul, we are told, "was very angry" (18:8). He "eyed David from that day on" (18:9), which is to say that Saul was envious of David from then on. First Samuel 18:10-11 shows how destructive jealousy (and fear; see 18:12) can be. For in these verses, we read that, "the next day," Saul was so disturbed that he went into a rage "while David was playing the lyre" and tried to kill David with a spear. "But David eluded him twice" (18:11b). In the passage for this lesson, Saul's plots to kill David continue. But fortunately, "the LORD was with" David (1 Samuel 18:12, 14).

1 Samuel 19:1-7

Saul's jealousy and fear of David became obsessive. The king spoke openly with his servants and his son Jonathan of his desire to kill David (19:1). So Jonathan decided to mediate on David's behalf with his father.

Jonathan did not immediately speak with his father on David's behalf. Instead, he first warned David to go into hiding until Saul's attitude softened (19:2-3). Then Jonathan went to try to dissuade his father from trying to kill David (19:4-5). And "Saul heeded the voice of Jonathan" (19:6a). The king took an oath and issued what seems to have been a royal declaration: "As the LORD lives, he [that is, David] shall not be put to death" (19:6b).

After securing David's safety, Jonathan went to where David was hiding and brought him back to the palace.

1 Samuel 19:8-17

Throughout these verses, we see a king bent on David's destruction. Saul's jealousy of David leads the king to forget his royal oath that he will not try to kill David. Repeatedly, he makes attempts on David's life. And repeatedly, David escapes.

Verses 8-10. For a parallel scene, see 18:10-11. The king sits in his house brooding over David's latest success in battle against the Philistines. David, the great warrior, is not concerned with battle, however, as he sits in Saul's house playing music to soothe the unstable king (see 16:23). Saul sits with a spear. David sits with a lyre (see 18:10). But as David affirmed to Goliath, "The LORD does not save by sword and spear" (17:47). The Lord is with David, and David eludes Saul's spear.

What is to be made of the references in 18:10 and 19:9 to "an evil spirit from God/the LORD" that "rushed upon" and "came upon" Saul? The account in 16:14-15 also speaks of "an evil spirit from the LORD" that tormented Saul after "the spirit of the LORD departed from Saul." Chapter 16 also tells of "the spirit of the LORD" coming "mightily upon David" when David was anointed king (16:13).

Saul's behavior when he is possessed by the "evil spirit from the LORD" appears to the modern reader to resemble the behavior of a person suffering from a severe psychological disorder. And, indeed, it was believed in the ancient world that psychological disorders were caused by evil spirits. The comment by the narrator that the evil spirit was "from God" or "from the LORD" seems to be a reflection of a belief that all things, good and bad, are subject to the will of God and that nothing can happen in the world unless God wills it, or, at least, allows it.

Verses 11-17. When Saul failed in his attempt to kill David with a spear, the king decided to send assassins to kill David at his home. But this time, David escaped with the help of his wife, Saul's daughter Michal.

When her father's henchmen came to kill David, Michal lowered her husband "down through the window; he fled away and escaped" (19:11-12). As we read this passage, we recall the story of how Rahab, a Canaanite woman who lived in Jericho, helped Joshua's spies escape capture by letting "them down by a rope through the window, for her house was on the outer side of the city wall and she resided within the wall itself" (Joshua 2:15). Perhaps the house of David and Michal, like Rahab's

DAVID'S MARRIAGE TO MICHAL, DAUGHTER OF SAUL

David was a close friend of Saul's son Jonathan (1 Samuel 18:1-4; 19:1-7). David also had another close link with the family of Saul. David was married to Michal, the younger of Saul's two daughters (14:49).

The story of David's marriage to a daughter of Saul begins during the Philistine war. Word was sent through the ranks of Israelite warriors that King Saul had promised his daughter in marriage to the man who killed Goliath (1 Samuel 17:25). The story of David's marriage to Michal is reported in 1 Samuel 18:17-28. The account concludes with the notice that Saul, knowing of Michal's love for David (18:28), "was still more afraid of David. So Saul was David's enemy from that time forward" (18:29). Thus, because of Saul's jealousy and fear of David, David's marriage to Michal did not begin under the best of circumstances.

Sadly, when David became a fugitive, Michal's father married her to another man (25:44). After David became king in Judah, he demanded that Michal be returned to him. Her second husband was greatly sorry to lose her (2 Samuel 3:12-16).

The marriage of Michal and David had a tragic ending. When David danced before the Lord as he was bringing the ark into Jerusalem, Michal was shocked and rebuked him. David rejected her and Michal died childless (2 Samuel 6:16-23).

house, was built right into the city wall. Therefore, when "Michal let David down through the window," she was actually letting David down on the outer side of the city wall. Being lowered from a window on the outer side of the city wall allowed David to escape into the countryside without passing through the main gate of the city where he could easily have been detected by Saul's assassins. (See also 2 Corinthians 11:32-33, where Paul reports that he once escaped capture in Damascus by being "let down in a basket through a window in the wall," and Acts 9:23-25.)

After lowering her husband through the window of their house, Michal tricked Saul's assassins into thinking that David was sick in bed, thereby giving David time to flee into the countryside. She put their household idol, frequently called in English translations a "teraphim" (TER-uh-fim), in David's bed, placed some goat hair on its head, and covered it with some clothes. In Genesis 31, we read of Laban's household idols or teraphim (see especially verses 19, 30, 34-35). While Laban's household idol was small enough to fit into a camel's saddle or cushion (verse 34), the teraphim in the home of David and Michal was large enough to pass for a grown man. The presence of such an idol in the home of David and Michal is somewhat surprising, since the worship of images and idols was prohibited in ancient Israel. *Teraphim*, in the centuries after the time of David, were specifically condemned as "abominations" (2 Kings 23:24).

When the idol in bedclothes was discovered and Saul inquired of his daughter why she had deceived him, Michal lied to her father. She claimed that David had threatened to kill her.

Is deception ever justified? Is it ever right to lie?

This story is designed to cast an unfavorable light on Saul and to elevate David. We see in Saul's plot the destructive results of obsessive envy and jealousy. And we see in Michal's actions a deep love and loyalty for her husband. But, as we read the story of Michal's idol in bedclothes, we wonder what a teraphim was doing in their home. And we wonder: Is deception ever justified? And is it ever right to lie?

Dimension 3:
What Does the Bible Mean to Us?

Dr. Judith Sills, in her bestseller *Excess Baggage*, lists "three great psychological poisons":

"1. Envy: The passionately unhappy feeling that you have something I don't have. And I want it!

"2. Jealousy: The sick and anxious hatred that floods my spirit when I fear that you want someone (or something) that I have. And you might get it!

"3. Inferiority: The secret dread one layer beneath my belief that I'm special. I'm not outstanding, I'm worthless."
(From *Excess Baggage: Getting Out of Your Own Way*, by Judith Sills, Ph.D.; Penguin Books, 1993; page 102.)

Let's consider what 1 Samuel 19 means to us in light of these "three great psychological poisons."

Envy. Our Scripture passage for this lesson, 1 Samuel 19:1-17, illustrates how destructive envy can be. Envy can destroy not only the psychological welfare of the person suffering under its influence. It can also destroy that person's friendships, marriage, and relationships with siblings.

It happens so often: People cannot be happy until they have what others have. Someone is not satisfied with his or her job because it does not pay as much or have the prestige or the perks that someone else's job offers. We are on a quest for "things" that someone else has with the hope that once we have what they have, we will be happy and fulfilled. If we cannot obtain the things that others have that we want, a destructive envy begins to burn within us that eats away at our sense of pride in who we are and keeps us from enjoying the life that we have.

I know a well-educated man who has a good-paying, stable job; a wonderful life; and the respect of his coworkers and clients. He is good at what he does and has achieved a margin of success in his field. And yet, so often he is fighting attacks of envy. For years, he has had his eyes on another job and that other job has always remained just beyond his grasp. There are times when the destructive powers of envy eat at him and try to convince him that he is "not good enough" because he does not have this other job. Sometimes his heart is breaking. Other times, like Saul, he is very angry (18:8) at those who have what he so desperately wants.

> Envy, jealousy, inferiority—three great psychological poisons that ruined Saul's life. Are they ruining yours?

It is my hope that my friend will be able to purge the psychological poison of envy from his life before the poison's powers destroy him and his relationships. Maybe, once he has purged the poison of envy from his life, he can truly be happy with what he has, who he is, and what he does.

Jealousy. Saul's jealousy of David was tormenting. The king focused on betrayal and loss. And instead of nurturing his relationships with his daughter and son-in-law, he sought to kill his son-in-law and ended up alienating his daughter.

Do you know someone like Saul? Or do you see yourself in Saul? Are you suffering from jealousy poisoning? I have known people in small town politics who, instead of focusing their attention on serving their constituents, have focused on ruining the reputations and careers of opponents—real or imagined. They had power, and they were sure that someone else wanted that power. They had an elected position, and they were sure that someone else wanted that position. The officeholders sacrificed their enjoyment of holding their positions to the poison of a jealous fear of losing those positions.

Inferiority. Throughout the saga of Saul's reign as the first king of Israel we see someone suffering from inferiority poisoning. I have known many people who are paralyzed by the hopelessness and uncertainty of inferiority—people who have grown up in abusive homes, people whose feelings of worth have been shattered by constant criticism and torment in abusive relationships, people whose feelings of worth have been shattered by unemployment.

How could Saul have purged from his life the "three great psychological poisons" of envy, jealousy, and inferiority? How can we save ourselves from the destructive powers of envy, jealousy, and inferiority? Dr. Sills observes, "You can best protect yourself from jealousy, envy, and inferiority by having a strong, realistic core of self-esteem" (page 103).

I wonder how Israelite history might have been different if King Saul had had adequate self-esteem to be able to accept David's success and fame. How might biblical history have changed if Saul, instead of feeling threatened by David because of the poisons of envy, jealousy, and inferiority, had had the self-esteem necessary to pursue a productive relationship with him? How might you be able to shape your life for the better by learning from Saul and purging your life of "the three great psychological poisons"? How might you be able to boost your self-esteem and to enjoy more fully the rich, abundant life that God wants you to live?

> "You can best protect yourself from jealousy, envy, and inferiority by having a strong, realistic core of self-esteem."

Dimension 4:
A Daily Bible Journey Plan

> *Day 1:* 1 Samuel 23
>
> *Day 2:* 1 Samuel 24
>
> *Day 3:* 1 Samuel 25:1-22
>
> *Day 4:* 1 Samuel 25:23-43
>
> *Day 5:* 1 Samuel 26
>
> *Day 6:* 1 Samuel 27:1–28:2
>
> *Day 7:* 1 Samuel 28:3-25

1 Samuel 24

7

DAVID SPARES SAUL'S LIFE

What to Watch For

Saul has been plotting to kill David. Now, however, Saul becomes vulnerable to attack from David.

• 1 Samuel 24:1-7. David has an opportunity to kill Saul. But David refuses to kill Saul. As you read this passage, watch for David's declaration of why he did not believe that it was proper for him to kill Saul.

• 1 Samuel 24:8-22. David confronts Saul. David informs Saul that he could have killed him but that he spared his life. As you study this passage, watch for David's declaration to Saul of his rationale for not killing him. Also, watch for Saul's response to David's declaration.

Dimension 1: What Does the Bible Say?

1. How do David's men interpret Saul's arrival in the cave where they have sought refuge, and what do they advise David to do? (1 Samuel 24:1-4a)

2. What does David do, and how does he feel afterward? (1 Samuel 24:4b-5)

3. Why does David not kill Saul? (1 Samuel 24:6)

4. What does Saul admit about David? (1 Samuel 24:17-20)

Dimension 2:
What Does the Bible Mean?

SETTING THE STAGE

At the end of the preceding lesson's Scripture passage, David has eluded Saul's attempts on his life and has fled into the countryside. Now David, a fugitive, becomes the leader of a renegade, outlaw militia, made up of "everyone who was in distress, and everyone who was in debt, and everyone who was discontented . . . ; and he became captain over them. Those who were with him numbered about four hundred" (1 Samuel 22:2). Saul, still obsessing in his jealousy and envy of David, is looking for David, hoping to find him and do away with him. David and his militia are camped at the "strongholds of En-gedi." And it is here, "in the wilderness of En-gedi," that the Scripture passage for this chapter picks up the story.

1 Samuel 24

As 1 Samuel 24 opens, Saul is informed of David's location. He is "in the wilderness of En-gedi [en-GED-igh]" (24:1). So, Saul heads out into the wilderness with "three thousand chosen men . . . to look for David and his men in the direction of the Rocks of the Wild Goats" (24:2).

THE WILDERNESS OF EN-GEDI

The Judean wilderness, the territory of Palestine just to the west of the Dead Sea, is one of the most forbidding, inhospitable plots of geography on earth. But in this hot, dry, barren wasteland is an oasis called En-gedi, "the most important and permanent of the several spring-fed oases that lay in antiquity below the cliffs of the wilderness of Judah on the W shore of the Dead Sea" (from *I Samuel,* Volume 8 of *The Anchor Bible* series, by P. Kyle McCarter, Jr.; Doubleday & Company, 1980; page 383). The name *En-gedi* means "Spring of the Young Goat." En-gedi is about halfway down the western shore of the Dead Sea and about thirty-five miles southeast of Jerusalem. The exact location of the "Rocks of the Wild Goats" is unknown; but it must have been in the vicinity of En-gedi, the "Spring of the Young Goat." Ibexes, a type of wild goat, can still be seen in the area of En-gedi.

Verse 3 of 1 Samuel 24 tells us that, while out hunting David, Saul paused "to relieve himself" (or "Saul went in to cover his feet," see the footnote in the New Revised Standard Version) in one of the many large caves that can be found in the cliffs in the Judean wilderness. It just so happens that David and his men had sought refuge in that same cave.

The caves of Palestine were frequently used as places of refuge for fugitives. For example, we saw in 1 Samuel 13:6 that, when the Israelites were fleeing before the mighty Philistine army, some of them "hid themselves in caves." Just about twenty miles north of En-gedi are the famous caves in the cliffs above Qumran where the Dead Sea Scrolls were hidden almost two thousand years ago and first began to surface again in 1947.

So, there were David and his men in one part of the cave and Saul, unaware of David's presence, in another part of the cave. David had the chance to kill Saul. He had the chance to kill the man who had been trying to kill him. David could have brought an end to his life as a fugitive and made a bid for the throne. And, indeed, David's men encouraged him to do just that. They suggested to David that he kill Saul while he had the chance. David's men interpreted Saul's wandering into the cave as a sign from God, as God giving Saul into David's hand (verse 4). And later, when David was talking with Saul, David himself suggested the possibility that it was God's will that Saul happened into the cave where David was hiding with his men (verse 10).

In 24:4, David's men declare that, "Here is the day of which the LORD said to you, 'I will give your enemy into your hand, and you shall do to

him as it seems good to you.' " There is no record in Scripture of such a promise from God. Perhaps David's men were just assuming that God had made such a promise to David. The crux of the passage is not in the first part—"I will give your enemy into your hand"—but in the second—"and you shall do to him as it seems good to you." What would seem to be the good thing to do to one's enemy? While certainly not a pacifist in his dealings with the enemies of Israel, David had a deep reverence and awe for "the LORD's anointed" (verses 6, 10), God's chosen one. Instead of killing Saul when he had the chance, David just cut off a part of Saul's robe. Later, David expressed remorse for having committed even that act against "the LORD's anointed" (verses 4b-6).

> David had a deep reverence and awe for "the LORD's anointed" and so would not kill Saul when the opportunity presented itself to David.

David persuaded his men not to kill Saul and reprimanded them for putting in his mind thoughts of violence against the Lord's anointed. The episode ended with Saul leaving the cave after his pause, unaware that anything had happened (verse 7b).

When Saul leaves the cave, David follows not far behind. David inquires of Saul why he listens to people who slander David (verse 9). Then, suggesting that it was God's will that they both ended up in the same cave, David explains to Saul that some of his men had urged him to kill the king. But David refused to yield to the temptation, affirming to Saul as he had to his men, that he would not strike down "the LORD's anointed" (verse 10). As proof of what he had just told Saul, David holds up "the corner of [Saul's] cloak." David points out to the king that because he only cut off a part of Saul's garment and did not kill him, Saul should know that "there is no wrong or treason in [David's] hands." David concludes by declaring, "I have not sinned against you, though you are hunting me to take my life" (verse 11). In verses 12 and 15, David invokes God as judge to determine whether he is guilty of treason or insurrection.

In 24:16-21, Saul responds to David's speech. First, in verses 17-19, Saul admits that David is "more righteous" than he. Saul affirms (verse 17) that David has repaid him with good, whereas he has repaid David with evil. In verse 19, Saul expresses his amazement at the way David has treated him, an enemy. "Who has ever found an enemy, and sent the enemy safely away?" Godly behavior frequently astonishes others. Expressions of grace often seem amazing.

> Godly behavior frequently astonishes others. Expressions of grace often seem amazing.

Second, in verses 20-21, Saul confesses and confirms what Jonathan had indicated in 1 Samuel 23:17. Saul is aware that David will be his successor on the throne and that only with David will the kingdom truly be established. This means that Saul, knowingly, is opposing the will of God.

At the end of the story of David's marriage to Saul's daughter Michal, the narrator declares that "Saul was David's enemy from that time forward" (1 Samuel 18:29b). Later, when Saul asked Michal why she helped David escape from Saul's assassins, Saul inquired of Michal, "Why have you deceived me like this, and let my enemy go, so that he has escaped?" (19:17). Saul clearly thought of David as his enemy.

With Saul's life in David's hands, David's men declared to their leader, "Here is the day of which the LORD said to you, 'I will give your enemy into your hand, and you shall do to him as it seems good to you'" (24:4). An engaging thought, indeed: You shall do to your enemy as it seems good to you. What would seem to be the good thing to do to one's enemy? David quoted an ancient proverb that declares that wickedness comes from those who are wicked (24:13). He refused to be ranked among the wicked, so he refused to act wickedly even against Saul.

What did it seem good for David to do to his enemy? Saul commented that David had repaid him good, whereas he had repaid David evil (24:17). Saul was absolutely astonished at how David treated him (24:19).

David lived out, and sets the example for, a fundamental principle of behavior taught by Jesus and Paul. In Matthew 5:43-48 and Luke 6:27-36, Jesus indicates that he expects his followers to love their enemies. If we just love those who love us, what is so special about that? Even sinners do that. Jesus expects more of his followers. Jesus expects his followers to practice higher standards of behavior and ethics. Jesus teaches his followers, "Love your enemies, do good to those you hate you, bless those who curse you, pray for those who abuse you" (Luke 6:27-28; see also Matthew 5:43-44).

> David lived out, and sets the example for, a fundamental principle of behavior taught by Jesus and Paul: do not repay evil with evil.

In Romans 12:17 and 1 Thessalonians 5:15, Paul challenges Christians to repay evil, not with more evil, but with good. This, of course, is the very behavior that Saul observed in David. Saul commented that David had repaid him with good, while he himself had repaid David with evil (24:17). A thousand years after the time of David, the apostle Paul taught the churches at Thessalonica and Rome that Christians should not repay evil done them with more evil, for that just perpetuates the cycle of evil. Rather, Christians should strive to do "to one another *and to all*" only those things that are good and noble (1 Thessalonians 5:15, italics added; see also Romans 12:17).

But oh, how difficult this is! How difficult it is to love our enemies, to

59

do good to those who hate us, to bless those who curse us, and to pray for those who abuse us. It is far easier to repay evil with more evil. Society expects us to follow the easy way. David's men seem to have expected their leader to return violence with more violence, to try to kill the one who had been trying to kill him, to behave as an enemy to the one who considered him an enemy, to repay evil with more evil, to join the ranks of the wicked, and to do wicked things. Saul was surprised when David did not act in this way. What kind of person finds an enemy, then lets the enemy go?

> Returning good for evil is amazing; loving even those who do not love you is astonishing. Such love is a sign of grace. It is nothing less than amazing grace.

Yes, returning good for evil is amazing. Loving even those who do not love you is astonishing. In fact, it is a godly trait. Such love is a sign of grace. It is nothing less than amazing grace.

Consider the example that David set for us and the implications for our lives of the remarkable teachings of Jesus and Paul. First, is it possible for a godly person to consider someone, anyone, an enemy? In his classic work *The Cost of Discipleship,* Dietrich Bonhoeffer writes, "In the New Testament our enemies are those who harbour hostility against us, not those against whom we cherish hostility, for Jesus refuses to reckon with such a possibility. The Christian must treat his enemy as a brother, and requite his hostility with love. His behaviour must be determined not by the way others teat him, but by the treatment he himself receives from Jesus" (from *The Cost of Discipleship*, by Dietrich Bonhoeffer; revised and unabridged edition; Macmillan, 1970; page 164).

Second, what would it mean for Saul to be David's enemy? What does it mean for someone to be our enemy to whom we are supposed to reach out in love? Again, we turn to Bonhoeffer's *Cost of Discipleship*: "By our enemies Jesus means those who are quite intractable and utterly unresponsive to our love, who forgive us nothing when we forgive them all, who requite our love with hatred and our service with derision. . . . Love asks nothing in return, but seeks those who need it. And who needs our love more than those who are consumed with hatred and are utterly devoid of love? Who in other words deserves our love more than our enemy?" (page 164).

David set the example. Jesus and Paul offered us the challenge. In family settings, where you work, in your business, in your school, in your clubs and organizations, on the street corners of the community where you live, in your church, love your enemies. Do good to those who hate you. Bless those who curse you. Pray for those who abuse you. Do not repay evil with evil. Rather, repay evil with good.

Day 1: 1 Samuel 29

Day 2: 1 Samuel 30:1-20

Day 3: 1 Samuel 30:21-31

Day 4: 1 Samuel 31

Day 5: 2 Samuel 1:1-16

Day 6: 2 Samuel 1:17-27

Day 7: 2 Samuel 2:1-17

**1 Samuel 31;
2 Samuel 1**

8

A Tragic Hero's End

What to Watch For

Saul had once stood "head and shoulders" above all Israel—their first
king, anointed by God's command. He had united their kingdom and, at
least for a while, had led them successfully in battle against the Philistines.
Now, Saul's kingship falls like a streaking meteor. His sons die in battle
before him. Then he takes his own life.

Read 1 Samuel 31 and 2 Samuel 1. Watch carefully how a suicide
occurs that may not have been necessary at all. Think about the internal
turmoil that Saul must have experienced as he watched his whole life
come unravelled around him on Mount Gilboa. Then examine the
response of David when he heard the news of Saul's death and, even
more, the news of the death of David's closest friend, Jonathan.

Let the story of Saul's tragic end be a history lesson, but even more
explore its implications for life today. People struggle with crisis, turmoil,
and tragedy in ways every bit as real as Saul's horrible moment on his
mountaintop of defeat.

1. At what precise point do the Philistines actually make their first, real contact with Saul on Mount Gilboa? (1 Samuel 31:8)

2. Who rescues the dead body of Saul, and why do they feel compelled to do so? (1 Samuel 31:11-13; also see 1 Samuel 11)

3. What motives might have existed in the mind of the Amalekite who brought David the news of Saul's death? How did he misjudge David? (2 Samuel 1:1-16)

4. What does David's outpouring of emotion over the deaths of Jonathan and Saul reveal about David's character?

Dimension 2:
What Does the Bible Mean?

The visit to the witch at Endor (1 Samuel 28) reveals only a small part of Saul's desperation. Haunting the back of his mind is Samuel's statement that he and his sons will die in battle (1 Samuel 15) as the armies of Israel are defeated by the powerful Philistines. Israel's glorious triumph on that day when the giant Goliath fell seems a million years ago. Now, spread out below Saul as he stands on Mount Gilboa is the pride of the Philistines, an army more dominant than any foe that Israel has ever faced.

Yet, Saul's desperation has not totally clouded his once brilliant mili-

> As Saul prepared to meet the Philistines on Gilboa, he was haunted by Samuel's statement that Saul and his sons would die in battle.

tary mind. Gilboa rises almost 1,700 feet above sea level. It stands above the Valley of Jezreel, one of the main northwest passageways into the Jordan Valley. Across the centuries, army commanders have fought on the Plains of Megiddo and then retreated to Mount Gilboa as an almost impregnable stronghold and last line of defense. Saul's plan is well-conceived. High ground always holds a distinct advantage.

As the Philistines look up to the high ridges of Gilboa, they know their work will not be easy. The king's colors are arrayed before them. His best soldiers, even his own sons, are by his side. Yet, if the Philistines can storm the mountaintop, the homeland that Israelites chased their forebears from centuries before might be theirs again. The valiant David and his feared armies are fighting elsewhere. Storming the mountain is a grave undertaking, but a battle won here will open an avenue into the heart of Israel. A valiant struggle like those at places such as Normandy, Gettysburg, or Missionary Ridge is about to take place at Gilboa. There will be a day of glory; assuredly, there will also be a day of death.

In the battles of Saul's day archers functioned like modern artillery. Thousands of arrows filled the skies before onrushing foot soldiers. First, the sky would be dark with arrows; and then the assault, the clashing charge of "infantry," would be unleashed.

While Saul's sons died in the wave of fighting unfolding before him on the lower reaches of the mountain, Saul was badly wounded by the archers. Whether his wounds were mortal is not clear. The Bible only indicates that he was badly wounded.

In his own mind, Saul knew what would happen next. The arrows would stop, and the Philistine swords would be upon him. He would be made into an object of brutal play as the Philistines taunted and tortured him. He was sure that in a moment he would be a living/dying battle trophy. So Saul commanded his armor-bearer to kill him, but the man refused. To take the life of God's anointed might bring a fate worse than death. Saul therefore fell on his own sword and took his life.

> Suicide ends the life force within human existence, and the dominant Hebrew view was that as long as that life force even barely glimmered there was hope.

Students of the Bible have debated whether to call Saul's death a suicide. Many cultures assert that death with dignity and honor surpasses the kind of end Saul probably rightly imagined the Philistines would bring to him. A captured Saul would have provided the Philistines with only an additional weapon to use against the Israelites.

Yet, suicide was never seen as an acceptable option in the Hebrew world.

Suicide assumed that all other options were closed and therefore ended any ability of people to find new possibilities for themselves or for God to come to people's rescue. Suicide ended the life force within human existence, and the dominant Hebrew view was that as long as that life force even barely glimmered there was hope. No discussion of suicide as sin is found here but rather almost a sadness about an event that did not have to occur.

More than anything, Saul's suicide may simply have been a needless alternative, a choice that in the longer view might not have been necessary at all. Here may be the key point to the recalling of Saul's tragic end on Gilboa. First Samuel 31:8 clearly states that on the day that Saul took his own life, the foot soldiers did not come as far as the mountaintop where Saul stood. The archers' arrows made it there, but the swordsmen never carried the crest of the hill. In exhaustion, they stopped their ascent. Not until the next day did the Philistines come to the top of the mountain to strip the dead and to take their spoils of war. Only then did they discover the dead body of Saul. It was not valiant soldiers who ultimately came to Saul but the cowardly stragglers after the camp who scavenged for spoils.

The point is clear: Saul assumed too much. He was convinced that the swords would be quick upon him, and they were not. Yes, he was wounded; but had he stayed his course, he probably would not have died on Gilboa. He could have lived to fight, to lead, another day. By taking his own life, all his options were surrendered. As with so many suicides, had Saul not jumped to tragic conclusions, whole new avenues of opportunity might have presented themselves.

> As with so many suicides, had Saul not jumped to tragic conclusions, whole new avenues of opportunity might have presented themselves.

With a savage and primitive brutality, the Philistines cut off Saul's head and then took his armor and body and placed them on public display. Such practices were commonplace in the warfare of that time. Messengers were sent throughout the land of the Philistines, and crowds gathered to celebrate the victory and to view the cruel trophies of war.

When the men of Jabesh-gilead heard of the desecration of Saul's body, they moved quickly to mount a special mission to reclaim their fallen hero's remains and those of his sons. The men of Jabesh-gilead felt a debt of obligation to Saul. In one of his first moments of public grandeur as king of Israel (1 Samuel 11), Saul broke an Ammonite siege of Jabesh-gilead. The men of the region, with honor and courage, did not forget.

The text says that the men of Jabesh-gilead burned the bodies of Saul and his sons and then buried their bones. This sort of cremation was not the typical way for Hebrews to deal with the dead. Burial of the entire body was customary. Some translators even suggest that the word translated "burn" should really be "anoint," describing the anointing with spices common to burial practices. More than likely, however, the idea of burning is accurate here. Had the Philistines discovered the whereabouts of Saul's grave, they would have exhumed the remains and repeated their desecrations.

Second Samuel begins with the news of Saul's defeat reaching David at Ziklag in the southwestern part of Palestine where he had just been successful in suppressing an Amalekite invasion. The grave news comes in the person of an Amalekite who has loyalties to Israel. Without question, the man feels that David will rejoice in the news of Saul's death. His story is exaggerated as he claims to have killed Saul himself. He even has Saul's crown and armlet as proof of his claim. He undoubtedly believes that he will be the recipient of some great acclaim and reward.

David, however, takes no joy in the deaths of Saul and his sons. There is no triumph in another person's tragedy. In fact, David has the Amalekite immediately killed for whatever role he has played in Saul's death or for his lying about Saul for his own gain.

> David's tribute recognized Saul's greatness, albeit a greatness that had been ravaged by emotional instability.

Second Samuel 1 concludes with a profoundly emotional lament by David for Saul and more especially for Jonathan. The "Book of Jashar" mentioned in the text must have been a collection of poetic manuscripts that no longer remains. The lament is highly personal. No theological overtones are included whatsoever, and God's name is not even mentioned. Without equivocation, David confesses a powerful love for Jonathan. He was as close as a brother, and the wonder of their relationship surpassed in David's poetic passion even the love he had known with women.

David also expresses deep affection for Saul. On one level, political conventionality had made them enemies and adversaries. Perhaps some forces beyond either of their control had forced them along contrary paths that, at least from Saul's perspective, were often filled with great rancor. On a deeper level, David saw beyond the Saul who fell into paranoia and jealousy. Theirs had been a clash of heroes, the titans of their day and time. David recognized Saul's greatness, albeit a greatness that had been ravaged by emotional instability. In this final moment of tribute, the best of Saul had to be remembered. The last line of the poetic elegy might read:

How the mighty have fallen,
    the heroes of war perished!

The Tragedy of Suicide

Suicide used to be a powerful exception in normal, everyday life. Now it has become altogether too commonplace. Almost everyone will know someone who has committed suicide or tried to. A great epidemic of suicide has reached into the lives of our teenagers and young adults. Suicide today has become an ever increasingly present national tragedy.

Conventional religious arguments against suicide have been less than effective. The typical argument that suicide is murder that cannot be forgiven and is therefore a sin that condemns a person to hell serves little redeeming purpose for that person whose life has become so desperate that no logic or sense can be found anymore.

The story of Saul at Gilboa, however, allows the Bible to provide a teaching about suicide that is compelling and decisive. Saul was in a terrible fix, and he rightly judged exactly what the Philistines would do to him if they captured him. The terror of exhausted possibilities ripped at Saul, and he took his own life. What he did not understand was that the charging armies of the Philistines were also exhausted. They had fought a destructive, uphill battle all day long. Their archers found the top of the mountain, but the foot soldiers never did. Yes, Saul was badly wounded; but if he had not given up and killed himself, yet unrealized options would have doubtless presented themselves.

To commit suicide is to close the door on all possibilities, to never have a chance to see "what might have been." Suicide is a total surrender of hope that life can be better, a total surrender of faith in oneself, others, and God. One wonders how many times suicides have occurred just on the eve, the horizon, of solution and answer.

> To commit suicide is to close the door on all possibilities, to never have a chance to see "what might have been."

A well-known poster shows a cat hanging on to a knot at the end of a rope. The caption reads: "When you have done all you know to do, tie a knot and hold on!" Yes, life had become totally absurd for Saul; but it might not have been the next day. He simply would not give this next day a chance to happen.

Does the reasoning of holding on for better options appeal to you? Could you use Saul's example to approach someone who might be talking about suicide? The Broadway musical character Annie asserts with great courage: "The sun will come out tomorrow!" Scarlett O'Hara in *Gone With the Wind* heroically proclaims: "Tomorrow is another day!"

The Failure of Others

Without doubt the conniving Amalekite felt he had a wonderful plan. David and Saul had become adversaries of the highest order, and now Saul was dead. David would surely celebrate Saul's death and defeat. The way to the throne of Israel was cleared for David. There had to be a reward for bringing such good news.

Instead, David was cut to the core of his emotions. He took no pleasure in someone else's failure. He saw Saul's death as a personal tragedy and a tragedy for the entire nation of Israel.

> Wishing an opponent injury or harm is a movement of immaturity and personal weakness, not a movement of emotional strength and character "wellness."

How difficult it is to show true compasssion for someone else's trouble. On the golf course, someone else's errant shot may mean that you will win the contest. Under your breath, have you ever taken joy in someone else's mistake or error? At a ballgame, have you ever been happy about a star player on the opponent's team being injured?

Although such thoughts are quite common, David would have nothing to do with them. If David were a coach, he would want his team to be at full strength and his opponent's team at full strength. He would want both sides to be at the top of their game. Only then would the competition be most legitimate. Jesus advised people to pray for those who used them (Matthew 5:43-44). Wishing an opponent injury or harm is a movement of immaturity and personal weakness, not a movement of emotional strength and character "wellness."

The "Manliness" of Love

The Bible is clear that David loved Jonathan. In fact, no other word but *love* could accurately describe their relationship. However, this does not mean that David was less than manly.

When did it become impossible for a man to express affection for another man without someone seeing impropriety or scandal? In some ways was David's culture more sophisticated in its approach to human interactions than our society?

David would not first have thought about Jonathan in terms of gender. Jonathan was a person with whom David shared comradeship, a bond of friendship, and a common history of mutual support. Jonathan was not first male or female; Jonathan was Jonathan. David emotionally grieved the loss of his closest friend; any concern for gender was beside the point.

Dimension 4:
A Daily Bible Journey Plan

Day 1: **2 Samuel 2:18-32**

Day 2: **2 Samuel 3:1-21**

Day 3: **2 Samuel 3:22-39**

Day 4: **2 Samuel 4**

Day 5: **2 Samuel 5:1-16**

Day 6: **2 Samuel 5:17-25**

Day 7: **2 Samuel 6:1-11**

A GRAND IDEA— REJECTED

What to Watch For

The people of Israel were gaining parity with their neighbors. They now had a king, armies led by that king and his commanders, even a king's house rising amidst the emerging skyline of the king's city—"The City of David"—Jerusalem. Only one element was lacking—a "house" for Israel's God. Other nations had their holy buildings, immaculate temples that asserted the grandeur of a people every bit as much as the grandeur of their deity. If everyone else had a "god place," Israel needed its own.

Read 2 Samuel 7. Take note of the role played by the prophet Nathan. Watch the way in which the focus of the text changes from a "house" for God to the promise of a Davidic dynasty that will rule over Israel for years to come. Be careful to observe the description that God gives of God's self.

Dimension 1: What Does the Bible Say?

1. Why does Nathan change his mind and advise David not to build a house for God? (2 Samuel 7:3-5)

2. What does 2 Samuel 7 say about God's need for a habitation to dwell in? (2 Samuel 7:6-7)

3. What does the passage say about who will build a house for God? (2 Samuel 7:12-13)

4. How does David respond to God's rejection of the plan for building a temple? (2 Samuel 7:18-29)

Dimension 2:
What Does the Bible Say?

SETTING THE STAGE

By approximately 1000 B.C., Palestine was dominated by three distinct political realities—the two southern tribes of Judah and Benjamin who had aligned themselves with David; the other ten tribes who had old alignments with Saul's family; and the city of Jerusalem, powerful enough in its own right to have independence and autonomy.

Following the death of Saul, a seven-year civil war was fought between the followers of David and the followers of Saul. Saul's son, Ishbaal (ISH-bay-uhl), nominally reigned over "Israel," that loosely connected confederacy of remaining tribes. Meanwhile David ruled Judah and Benjamin from Hebron.

After seven years of fighting, the house of Saul became weaker and weaker while the house of David grew more powerful. Finally, the leaders of Israel (2 Samuel 5:1-3) went to David at Hebron and made him their king. Two sides of the Palestine triangle of power were in place. David next moved quickly to capture Jerusalem, triumphantly bringing the sacred ark of the covenant into the city and establishing his own house (2 Samuel 5:6-10; 6).

Second Samuel 7 describes the beginning of a rest from fighting. In the period of peace that was dawning, new priorities could come into view. As David surveyed his new situation and began to think about what he might do next, it occurred to him that he had a dwelling place but that the ark of the covenant—the physical symbol of God's presence with the people—still was protected only by a tent.

David saw the need for a "House of God," a temple where the ark could be stored and worship of God given central focus in Jerusalem.

A "House of God," a temple where the ark could be stored and worship of God given central focus in Jerusalem, was needed. In fact, there was a precedent for building such a structure. At Shiloh in central Palestine north of Jerusalem a place referred to as the "house" of God or "temple" of God had been used earlier as a worship center and a place to keep the ark of the covenant. Eli the priest had served there. Hannah brought her son Samuel to this site as a gift to the service of God (1 Samuel 1).

No motives are probably totally pure. David likely came to the idea of a temple project from several perspectives. He may have felt that it was not fair for him as king to have a dwelling place and God somehow to be left out. The building of a permanent worship site would also be a thanksgiving offering to God for the success he had helped David secure. More than anything else, the Temple would be David's gift—Israel's gift—to God.

Jerusalem was a hub city of the entire Middle East. The Temple here would make an unmistakable statement about Israel's God. An overwhelming and magnificent building in Jerusalem would convey the power of David's God

David may also have had some pragmatic reasons for the building of a temple. Jerusalem was a hub city of the entire Middle East. The world's paths crisscrossed at Jerusalem. The people passing through were influenced by every kind of religion, every kind of religious leader, and every kind of religious building imaginable. The Temple would make an unmistakable statement about Israel's God. An overwhelming and magnificent building in Jerusalem would convey the power of David's God.

Without question, a building project the likes of which Jerusalem had probably never seen would add to the personal stature of David. When rulers came to power in those days—and this fact is probably true of most human history—they tended to become involved in gigantic building projects as a statement of their own power and prestige. Grand-scale building projects became monuments to these rulers that would herald their power across the centuries. The Egyptian pharaohs of Moses' day built entire treasure cities as a statement to the world of their power and wealth. A temple project in Jerusalem would only heighten David's dominance.

For whatever combination of reasons, David conveyed his idea to the court prophet, Nathan. Most kings had court prophets who acted as advisors. Sometimes these prophets were little more than religious "yes men" who gave royal decisions religious credibility in the eyes of the general population. Later kings in Hebrew history kept hundreds of these prophets and surrounded them with enough "perks" that they always supported royal agendas no matter how insane they might be.

Although the prophet Nathan takes part in only two stories in Second Samuel (Chapters 7 and 12), he appears to have been close beside the king until the time of David's death (1 Kings 1–2). Nathan must have cared deeply about David, so deeply that he was never hesitant to confront the king about his excesses and failures. At first, Nathan seems like the typical cult prophet: the king wants to build a house for God, so Nathan gives approval. But the voice that dominates Nathan's life is God's voice. When God reveals that David is not to build the Temple, Nathan quickly comes to David with a new word. Nathan is not David's prophet but rather God's prophet.

How important it was for David to somehow recognize the vital need for a voice of dissent and opposition, even at the heart of his court. "Yes men" only dilute truth. David must have frank honesty, and Nathan became that voice of undiluted truth and total honesty. David was a real human being who made more than his share of critical, even moral, mistakes. He was not, however, a tyrant who abolished and prevented voices of truth. By preserving Nathan's role, David retained contact with God.

> David was a real human being who made more than his share of critical, even moral, mistakes. He was not, however, a tyrant who abolished and prevented voices of truth. By preserving the prophet Nathan's role, David retained contact with God.

Some biblical characters never achieve the limelight of center stage, but they nonetheless play vital roles. Jethro, Moses' father-in-law, was Moses' mentor and advisor from the time Moses was exiled from Egypt until the children of Israel wandered in the wilderness beyond Sinai. The quality of Moses' leadership was tremendously enhanced by Jethro's wisdom and insight. Nathan, without question, was a similar figure, behind the scenes but at the center of the best years of Israel's monarchy under David and the early years of the reign of Solomon.

Within God's communication through Nathan are decisive statements God is making about God's self. God explains that from the time God brought the people up from Egyptian bondage that God had been "moving about in a tent." In all places God had "moved about among all the people of Israel." There is even a specific word for David personally: "I have been with you wherever you went." God specifically makes the point that God has never asked for a permanent dwelling.

Is it possible that God was trying to convey the idea that a permanent dwelling is not the best expression of who God is? God cannot be confined or attached to one place. God is everywhere there are people in need. People do not have to come to God at a certain place; God comes to people where they are. The psalmist believed God would be with him "even though I walk through the darkest valley" (Psalm 23:4). Near the end of the Book of Revelation, the word is proclaimed:

> "See, the home of God is among mortals.
> He will dwell with them;
> they will be his peoples,
> and God himself will be with them." (Revelation 21:3)

> **God cannot be confined or attached to one place. God is everywhere there are people in need.**

The message of the indwelling of the presence of God with human beings is a profound message, the centerpiece of 2 Samuel 7. The text then moves off into what perhaps may be a much less important matter. At the end of the chapter is added a glowing statement about the way in which God will "build a house"—that is, establish a dynasty—for David. The text provides a compelling justification, in the words of God, for a succession of Davidic kings who will rule over Israel in the future. The emphasis at the end of the chapter on the way that the house of David will be blessed "forever" has led many interpreters to a messianic interpretation, although Hebrew messianic thought during the time of David would have been tremendously rare.

The careful reader should keep in mind that biblical texts can be used to advance important strategies. The strategy at the end of 2 Samuel 7 is to secure the reign of David's direct descendants as the rightful, God-authorized rulers of Israel. That God's "house" is finally to be built by a descendant of David gives even greater credibility to the Davidic dynasty.

Do not get too caught up in the issues of rightful kingship descending from David. The larger passage is filled with important meaning. In Nathan, an authentic, courageously honest prophet of God is encountered. In God's own words about the lack of necessity of a dwelling place being built, a deep insight into the character of God is revealed, precisely like that insight delivered by Jesus when he proclaimed: "And remember, I am with you always, to the end of the age" (Matthew 28:20b).

The Examined Life

People seldom have trouble deciding what they think they want to do. Often decisions are made quickly and haphazardly, without the benefit of weighing alternatives and understanding implications. Who among us has not failed to look before we have leaped?

David, on the spur of the moment, decided it was a good idea to build a temple for God. He did not stop to think about all the implications. In fact, he was thinking for God without giving God the opportunity of any input. Do we ever find ourselves deciding for our friends, our mates, our children, or our entire family where we are going to eat, what movies will be seen, the site for this year's vacation, what gift should be given on a special occasion? Maybe we should ask others what they might like to do before we forge ahead.

David, at least, had one saving grace—an advisor who took time to seek the will of God and to think about implications. More importantly, David had an advisor in Nathan who was a true friend, a person who would be totally honest with David rather than someone who would tell David what he thought David wanted to hear.

> Forging ahead without thinking, without praying for and seeking God's will, may promote that which, by contrast, is worthless.

Examining interpersonal relationships to Nathan-like friends and associates is of utmost importance. "Yes men" in business or even persons in families who are conflict-avoidant do us few favors. How much it matters when there are those who love us enough to be completely honest with us.

The ancient Greek philosophers believed that "the unexamined life is not worth living." In like manner, the unexamined relationship might not be worth entering into or the unexamined profession not worth pursuing. There may be a direct relationship between careful examination and worth. Forging ahead without thinking, without praying for and seeking God's will, may promote that which, by contrast, is worthless.

A Self-disclosure

At a few, central times in the Bible, God is not being talked about by others but seems to be talking about God's self. By comparison, what theologians have said about God over the centuries is not nearly as important as what God might say about God's self.

In Genesis 12, God tells Abram at Ur, very simply, that if Abram will follow, God will show him where to go. Later, at the burning bush

(Exodus 3), God conveys to Moses that God is aware of people in trouble and that God will move to liberate people from oppression and bondage. It is also clear from the choice of Abram and Moses that God is a God who works through human beings. In Luke 4, Jesus discloses to the people in his hometown of Nazareth that he is interested in preaching good news to the poor, releasing captives, bringing sight to the blind, and giving liberty to those who are oppressed. In passages like these, the "heart" of God is laid bare.

> In a mobile society that races at breakneck speed, how reassuring to hear that God moves along with people.

How compelling is the image drawn in 2 Samuel 7 of a God who will not be confined to any specific place but rather simply wants to be with people where they are. In a mobile society that races at breakneck speed, how reassuring to hear that God moves along with people. God must be quick to keep up with us, but we can be confident that God is sufficient for the task.

This self-disclosure of God's constant presence with the people is confirmed in Jesus' encounter with the woman at the Samaritan well described in John 4. The woman raised the theological issue of where God should be worshiped. Was Jerusalem the only appropriate place to worship God, or were the mountain sanctuaries legitimate holy places? Jesus totally resisted the idea that any ceiling can be built over God. For Jesus, "God is spirit" (verse 24) and can be encountered anywhere that people seek God on the "spiritual" level of their life. The God of Jesus and of 2 Samuel 7 resists definition, defies labeling, and can never be captured in a theological cubbyhole.

> A religious scholar once said that he did not always know what to believe but he did know with certainty where he should be—beside his neighbor in joy and in pain.

If these assessments of God are so powerfully insightful about God's nature, what can be said about people who would want to be "godly"? If God's emphasis is on being with people, should simply being with others in times of need become a leading characteristic of a "godly" person? A religious scholar once said that he did not always know what to believe but he did know with certainty where he should be—beside his neighbor in joy and in pain.

Finally, if God resists definition and labeling, should the legitimately "godly" person move away from that which stereotypes or caricatures human beings? If the "spirit" of God cannot be captured in a place, can the "spirit" of a person be limited by uninformed racism, sexism, or prejudice?

And if God "moves" with us, how can we be more sensitive to those "movings"? How can our faith be undergirded and bolstered by the positive realization that God is always there for us and with us in our world?

76

Day 1: 2 Samuel 6:12-23

Day 2: 2 Samuel 7:1-17

Day 3: 2 Samuel 7:18-29

Day 4: 2 Samuel 8

Day 5: 2 Samuel 9

Day 6: 2 Samuel 10:1-14

Day 7: 2 Samuel 10:15-19

2 Samuel 11:1–12:15a

10

DAVID AND BATHSHEBA

What to Watch For

In David's emotional elegy over Saul and Jonathan in 2 Samuel 1, he grieves over the fact that "the mighty have fallen." Read 2 Samuel 11:1–12:15a and notice how times of peaceful ease can be as filled with dangerous pitfalls as times of great adversity. David "falls" but not on a mountaintop of military conflict. He, instead, is defeated by his own lack of control, perhaps a sense that he is above the law, and poor choices made in the heat of a moment of lust-filled temptation. Note carefully how one misplaced instance of self-gratification can lead to a chain reaction of terrible events in which innocent people are compromised and even destroyed. No doubt, David did try valiantly at times to be a "man of God." His vulnerability that found expression in the affair with Bathsheba stands as a poignant reminder that we are all vulnerable when it comes to the making of poor choices and the lack of control of our behaviors.

Dimension 1:
What Does the Bible Say?

1. When did David's lustful thoughts about Bathsheba become sin? (2 Samuel 11:2-5)

2. What was Bathsheba's part in the unfolding of the events that took place? (2 Samuel 11:2-5, 26-27)

3. What is the significance of Bathsheba's "purifying" herself? (2 Samuel 11:4; see Leviticus 15)

4. How does the biblical writer understand the death of the child conceived in David and Bathsheba's lust? (2 Samuel 12:14)

Dimension 2:
What Does the Bible Mean?

Springtime had come to Israel and with it a traditional time for warfare and battle. In this particular spring no great invasions or defensive campaigns were demanded. The king's presence with his troops was not necessary. More than likely, minor incursions on Israel's frontiers were being beaten back. Israel's armies were serving notice to any potential interlopers that her forces were alive and well, ready to resist with full malice even the slightest aggression into her territory. David was at ease, a man of action perhaps a little bored with his daily routines. Sometimes adversity and strife give greater structure and discipline to life than ease.

79

The military information in this particular text is, however, secondary. A general setting is provided for the events that take place. Foremost in the biblical writer's mind is establishing the basic explanation, the primary causes, for the eventual and awful breakdown of David's family. That story will follow in later chapters of Second Samuel, and it will indeed be terrible and demand explanation. The explanation begins with David and Bathsheba.

"THE FORCE"

The famous series of *Star Wars* movies advanced the idea that there is a "dark side" of what is known as "The Force," the individual and corporate power of personality that drives human action. The evil character Darth Vader is the stark personification of that dark side. But, true *Star Wars* fans know that originally Darth Vader was a heroic Jedi knight motivated by goodness and ethical courage. At the end of his existence, Darth Vader was basically "saved" by the love of his son, Luke Skywalker, and embraced goodness in his dying moment and spiritual afterlife.

At some point, however, Darth Vader had turned to the dark side of "The Force." There is no good explanation why; perhaps there never is. The potential for goodness and evil is always there. Moral vulnerability is continual in life, and its implications are as close as a person's next poor decision. Darth Vader and David are timeless examples of the struggle between good and evil that is the lot of all human beings. David also demonstrated the ability to turn in a moment to the dark side of his existence.

Late one afternoon David was walking on the roof of the king's house. His elevated vantage point allowed him to look over into what was probably the inside courtyard of a neighboring dwelling. Bathsheba was bathing there. Of course, Bathsheba had the right to bathe within the privacy of her own home; but she would probably have been aware of the line of sight between her bath spot and the king's roof. The Bible does not indicate enticement on her part, but there is no indication of reasonable discretion either.

David was struck by Bathsheba's appearance. He then went beyond what he was thinking about Bathsheba in his mind and started making conscious inquiries about who she was. After he found out she was married, David took the next, conscious step of sending messengers to bring her to his house. He might not have been able to harness his thoughts, but he certainly was capable of managing the actions of inquiry and pursuit.

Bathsheba was as well; there is no report of the messengers forcing her to go to the king's house.

Maybe David had nothing more in mind than a "friendly visit." Perhaps Bathsheba had a natural curiosity about what the inside of the king's house was like. Perhaps the invitation was a form of flattery her ego could not resist. Yet, one thing led to another; and before they knew what happened basically natural events took an unconstrained course. David and Bathsheba broke faith with their mates, their own best selves, and the commandments of God.

Second Samuel 11:4b seems to provide an unnecessary aside that is not integral to the story. The text says Bathsheba "was purifying herself after her period." This statement found in the Jewish laws probably relates to the purification rituals involving the completion of a menstrual cycle (Leviticus 15:19-24). The biblical writer may be creating a stark contrast, which heightens the effect of what David and Bathsheba have done. She has been careful to bathe in order to remove her uncleanness following her "discharge of blood" but has callously, seemingly thoughtlessly, broken the commandment of God.

> How could a person, almost without conscience, break the commandment and yet observe the small details of the cleanliness ritual?

How could a person, almost without conscience, break the commandment and yet observe the small details of the cleanliness ritual?

A child is conceived, and now David is caught. A person might reply, "So what?" David was the king. An event like this would probably cause only a small ripple on the surface of his day. Few persons if any could argue with whatever liberties he might take. Instead, David dug his hole a little deeper. To cover his tracks, Uriah (yoo-RIGH-uh) the Hittite— Bathsheba's lawful husband—was basically murdered. It is amazing how much energy David gave to prevent being caught. He worried more about personal reputation than human life.

The details of Uriah's "murder" show how evil can reproduce itself. Uriah's goodness and dedication to David and Israel is conveyed in his refusal to spend the night with his wife while his comrades are still in battle. David's only remaining option is to write a message to his army commander, Joab (JOH-ab), that Uriah is to be placed at the forefront of the battle where he is almost bound to be killed and to have the letter carried to Joab by Uriah himself. Joab's cleverly devised battle strategy leaves several soldiers too close to the enemy city and in range of the archers on the wall. Uriah and several other men die. Totally innocent lives are adversely affected, and Joab is drawn into what now is a conspiracy of evil. David then coldly communi-

> David spent an amazing amount of energy to prevent being caught. He worried more about personal reputation than human life.

cates to Joab after the news of the battle and the deaths is received: "Do not let this matter trouble you, for the sword devours now one and now another." In other words: "So, a few men die in battle? Don't worry about it. No big deal!" To cover David's wrong, the value of human life is totally debased.

Almost without exception, secrets like those of David and Bathsheba do not stay hidden. There is no specific explanation for how the secret gets out; but these kinds of secrets can seldom be held, no more than a sieve can hold water. Allow yourself to be vulnerable in this particular manner, and it will be found out; you can count on it.

Once again Nathan appears. He loves David and cares for the monarchy, enough that he speaks the unadulterated truth. In Nathan's speech one finds the highest form of prophetic parable. The prophet weaves a story about a rich man who owns great flocks of sheep, yet to supply his own banquet table butchers the single ewe lamb of a poor man. The details of the parable draw out deep emotions—the lamb belongs to the poor man's children; it is more like a child itself than an animal.

The parable has the desired effect. David is overwrought. All at once, David is king, judge, and executioner. He decrees that the man will repay fourfold. No, the man will die! He has shown no pity.

> David brought condemnation upon himself without realizing it. All that Nathan had to say was: "David, you are the man!"

Nathan now has David exactly where he wants him. David brings condemnation upon himself without realizing it. All that Nathan has to say is: "David, you are the man!"

The crushing reality of David's sin with Bathsheba finds the light of day. David is caught. More precisely, David has caught himself. The questions come one after the other: What about the families of the men who died beside Uriah? What about the way that David has lost esteem and integrity in the eyes of his old friend, Joab? What about the way that David will never be able to deny and block out these events as long as he lives?

David's "punishment" will be vast: the sword will never depart from his own house; evil will rise toward him from within his own family; his wives will be taken by his neighbors; his child by Bathsheba will die. David cries out to God in confession, and God "puts away" his sin. Nevertheless, the text says, the implications of the evil cannot be retrieved.

At What Point Is It Sin?

Say to someone: "Do not think about a red elephant!" What happens?
Inevitably and immediately, the image of a giant red elephant jumps right
into the brain. How would it be possible for anything else to occur?

David saw a beautiful woman bathing in her courtyard. Could you
expect him not to notice? How reasonable would it be to think that sensual
thoughts would not rise in his mind?

Jesus taught that what one thinks in one's heart defines to a large extent
one's character (Matthew 15:18-19). Perhaps Jesus would distinguish
between passing thoughts and obsessive ones. Uninvited, passing thoughts
do not define character; pursued, obsessive ones certainly do. Jesus also
said that thinking something in your heart in the way of lust is the same as
actually committing the act (Matthew 5:28). Such "lust-filled" thinking
often involves strategies and actions that would bring the thoughts to
reality.

David sinned when he began consciously and strategically to act on his
thoughts. Prior to his specific actions, his thoughts could have been controlled and limited. No real harm would have been done, and David would
probably have been a morally stronger man.

Jesus also taught that it is not what goes into a
person that corrupts him or her but what comes out
(Matthew 15:17-18). A person may not be able to
control a passing thought that comes into the
mind, but what is done with that thought in terms
of action is a matter of choice. The conscious decisions that drive our actions make us responsible.
When the actions of our life shirk this responsibility, sin enters the picture.

> A person may not be
> able to control a
> passing thought that
> comes into the mind,
> but what is done with
> that thought in terms
> of action is a matter
> of choice.

Shared Blame

Is David the absolute culprit in this story, or does Bathsheba carry part of
the blame for what took place? Did Bathsheba demonstrate adequate resis-
tance to David's advances? Could she have just said no? What is the status
of saying no in our modern relationships? How far would David have gotten with the modern argument: "Oh yeah, she said 'no,' but I could tell
that her 'no' really meant 'yes,' and she wanted me to press on!"?

Does any shared blame extend to Joab for his blind loyalty to David?
Joab knew what was happening but never even slightly questioned

David's plan, even though he had to know innocent people would die. When have we followed the plans of powerful persons without questioning their motives?

Close the Barn Door

An old cliché conveys the wisdom that once the horse is stolen from the barn, it does little good to worry about closing the door. The story of David and Bathsheba should be read by anyone contemplating or planning an affair who thinks he or she can be discreet and secretive enough to never be caught. Most affairs happen in perfect parallel to this biblical precedent. The numerical percentage of those who "get caught" must be nine out of ten.

Then, there is the hurt that begins to spread like wildfire and seldom ever goes completely away. To follow the cliché, the only way to keep the horse securely in the barn is to keep the door carefully closed. Strict, uncompromising parameters on certain actions prevent a painful chain of falling dominoes from ever beginning to drop.

When the long course of David's life is seen and the awful implications of this affair are surveyed, what might David say about the "worth" of his involvement with Bathsheba? If he was like most people caught up in the hurtful aftermath of this kind of infidelity, there is probably no question; it simply was not worth it.

The Punishment of God

Without question, in the early periods of Israel's history, almost any negative event was seen as some sort of punishment from God. This text supports the idea of God as such a punishing God. The baby's death is directly caused by David's sin. God brings about the baby's death as a specific punishment.

> In the early period of Israel's history, almost any negative event was seen as some sort of punishment from God. Christians believe that viewing negative events in terms of God's punishment is outdated, that each person bears responsibility for his or her own sins.

Many people still hold strongly to this idea. If something bad happens in their lives, they understand this "bad" as a punishment for something they have done wrong. The problem comes when genuinely good persons experience great negatives in life. They are left wondering what they did that has brought the punishment. Deep confusion about one's relationship with God can be the result.

The idea that God would take the life of an innocent baby because of the sins of that baby's parents is hard to reconcile with the loving, caring God revealed in Jesus Christ. The solution to this dilemma might be that the theology reflected in Second Samuel is quite primitive. The prophet Jeremiah, who lived several centuries after David, taught that a new covenant era was about to dawn (Jeremiah 31:29-34) in which each person would bear responsibility for his or her own sins. We believe that that era has arrived and that viewing negative events in terms of God's punishment is outdated in our time.

Dimension 4:
A Daily Bible Journey Plan

Day 1: 2 Samuel 11:1-13

Day 2: 2 Samuel 11:14-27a

Day 3: 2 Samuel 11:27b–12:15a

Day 4: 2 Samuel 12:15b-25

Day 5: 2 Samuel 12:26-31

Day 6: 2 Samuel 13:1-22

Day 7: 2 Samuel 13:23-39

2 Samuel 13

11

*I*T'S A FAMILY TRADITION

What to Watch For

The title of this chapter is from a country music song by Hank Williams, Jr. In the song, Hank, Jr. talks about the fast-track, hard-living existence that he has pursued across his life. As he describes it, there has been more than enough turmoil and trouble for several lifetimes. Hank, Jr. has, however, only been following a "family tradition," trying to mirror the actions of his legendary father.

Read 2 Samuel 13 to discover to what extent David's children were following their "family traditions" for negative living and poor decision-making. Although David did many wonderful things for Israel and in the name of God, evidently his neglect of family and poverty of proper relationship examples had a powerful, negative influence on his children. Sometimes it seems that negative examples have more power in the influencing of children than positive ones. In this chapter we encounter only the beginning of the horrific implications of David's sin with Bathsheba.

Dimension 1:
What Does the Bible Say?

1. How would you make a comparison between the events surrounding David and Bathsheba and those involving Amnon and Tamar? (2 Samuel 11; 2 Samuel 13)

2. What happens after Amnon is successfully intimate with Tamar? (2 Samuel 13:15-22)

3. How did Absalom take revenge on his brother Amnon? What was the result of his action? (2 Samuel 13:23-29)

4. What was David's role in this situation? What did he do about the events that were taking place in his family? (2 Samuel 13:21, 30-31)

Dimension 2:
What Does the Bible Mean?

The precise number of wives and children David had is not known. At least eight different women are named as being wives of David and, depending on which list is consulted, he had as many as nineteen sons. Daughters, except for Tamar (TAY-mahr), are not named. The "great man" theory that was operative in primitive civilizations encouraged a man like David to have as many children as possible. The general population of a nation could be enhanced by numerous offspring of a "great man." Many of the wives would have been part of alliances and treaties struck with other nations. Having children for a man of David's position could easily have lost all emotion and sense of responsibility. Raising these children he sired would have to be someone else's duty.

Amnon (AM-non) was David's first noted son, borne to him by a woman named Ahinoam (uh-HIN-oh-um) of Jezreel. The standard premise of that ancient world was that Amnon, being the first-born, had all the rights to be crown prince and, at his father's death, to become king over Israel. Early in his life, Amnon was undoubtedly being groomed for this position.

> **When power is at stake, family loyalty often takes on a low priority.**

In the king's house were all kinds of half brothers and half sisters whose mothers were from different countries, often countries that had long-established hatreds for one another. Therefore, there was always some intensity of palace intrigue as mothers and children competed for positions of advantage and David's favor. Half brothers especially competed blatantly for special status in their father's eyes. Sometimes that competition knew no bounds. When power is at stake, family loyalty often takes on a low priority.

No one was more ambitious for power than David's third son, Absalom (AB-suh-luhm). His claims for attention were more than justified; he was handsome, a good leader, and beloved by his father; he had proved himself highly capable at military strategy. But Absalom was not to be king. Then, David's second child, Chileab (KIL-ee-ab, or Daniel) died; and the only person standing in the way of Absalom and kingship was Amnon. Do not be too easily convinced that what Absalom did to revenge the rape of Tamar was for Tamar alone and not for himself.

> **Amnon became desperately attracted to a beautiful woman and began to lose all semblance of reasonable thinking.**

Exactly like his father before him, Amnon became desperately attracted to a beautiful woman and began to lose all semblance of reasonable thinking. His greatest problem, however, was that the beautiful woman he fell in love with was his half sister and Absalom's full sister, Tamar. Tamar had close contact with her brother Absalom, who was intent on doing anything necessary to make Tamar happy and secure. To harm Tamar guaranteed Absalom's scorn and certain revenge.

Amnon was so obsessed with Tamar's beauty that be was becoming physically ill over not being able to have sex with her. Amnon had absolutely no desire to marry Tamar, even though marriage to half sisters was permissible and David's blessing for a marriage probably could have been gained. Amnon simply wanted her sexually.

A man named Jonadab (JOH-nuh-dab) entered the picture. He was David's nephew, a self-serving man only out for his own ambitions. He devised a plan for Amnon that would fulfill Amnon's wishes about Tamar. More than likely, Jonadab was trying to get into the good graces of the next king of Israel. The Bible identifies Jonadab simply as "a very crafty man." He was certainly more concerned with his own agenda than with any harm that might come to Tamar. He is as much of a culprit in this story as her rapist half brother.

Amnon was instructed to feign illness. When he did, David evidently wanted to help if there was anything he could do. He honored the strange request that Tamar prepare food for Amnon. In the midst of Tamar's ministrations the supposed sick man forced himself on her. She then begged Amnon to get David's blessing on a marriage, but all Amnon was interested in was sex. He forcibly raped her.

No sooner was the act of sexual violence completed than Amnon literally had Tamar thrown out of his house. The text reads: "Amnon was seized with a very great loathing for her; indeed, his loathing was even greater than the lust he had felt for her" (2 Samuel 13:15). Tamar begged for mercy. As bad as the rape was, the horror of being turned out into the community in a way that made her look like the villain rather than the victim was even more terrible. Amnon's servant literally threw Tamar onto the street and bolted the door behind her. Tamar was publicly humiliated. Amnon got all that he wanted and, having had his way with Tamar, tossed her aside.

The rape may have been more of a political act than it was a sexual act. Amnon successfully delivered a blow against his rival Absalom, declared himself the winner, and rid himself of Tamar. Insult and offense were added to injury.

> The rape of Tamar may have been more of a political act than it was a sexual act.

Her virginity was ruined, and Tamar was rendered almost unsuitable for marriage at all. Absalom came to his sister's aid and gave her refuge. About all David did, according to 2 Samuel 13:21, was to become "very angry." His anger, however, did nothing at all constructive to better the situation.

Absalom, however, was consumed with a desire for revenge. He did not even speak to Amnon for two years. Finally, Absalom held a sheepshearing at Baal-hazor (bay-uhl-HAY-zor) near Ephraim; and all his brothers—including Amnon—were invited. Sheepshearings were times of great frivolity, so some of the party may have felt that Absalom was trying to prepare for peace between himself and his brother. Nothing could have been further from the case. By a prearranged signal, Absalom's servants drew their weapons and killed Amnon.

Tamar's honor had been revenged, and Absalom's status as crown prince had become completely secure. Absalom went into exile for three years, however, perhaps fearing that he might become the object of revenge himself. The family at least seemed to surround Tamar with their love and support: Absalom gave her refuge and named his daughter after her (2 Samuel 14:27), while later Solomon buillt a city and named it after her (1 Kings 9:17-18).

Rumors reached David that Absalom had killed all his sons. Evidently, David must have felt that Absalom was capable of such an act; for he immediately showed abject grief by tearing his garments and lying on the ground (2 Samuel 13:31). In verses 36-37, David cries with relief and sorrow over the fact that Amnon is dead but his other sons are alive. He also eventually begins to yearn for Absalom's return. Note that when it comes to his family, David only has emotional responses—anger, grief, longing. He seems incapable of acting

> David, a man of such masterful action in political and military arenas, seemed handicapped when it came to his family. Perhaps he was "too busy otherwise" to learn how to deal with family matters.

decisively and reasonably to help or resolve his family's problems. How could a man of such action in political and military arenas be so handicapped when it came to his family? Perhaps, David never acted decisively on family matters because he was so busy otherwise. When the need to act came, he simply did not know how.

Jonadab, ever the opportunist, was nearby when the rumored news of the death of all David's sons came. Such self-serving opportunists almost always seem to be "nearby." He knew all about Absalom's plan to kill Amnon; in fact, given his past performance with Amnon, he may have contributed to the plan. Had he seen any advantage in helping Absalom, even if it cost his old friend Amnon his life, Jonadab would not have hesitated for a moment to help.

Now, Jonadab saw a chance to gain David's favor. Almost like a seer, he told David that only Amnon had died. There are plenty of people in the world like Jonadab, playing whatever angle gives them advantage, knowing no loyalty to friends, and willing to find any means to further their ends. Perhaps the bib-

> Is it possible to love too much and to become blind to the way that love can be abused?

lical writer wove his characterization of Jonadab into this larger story so that people might be carefully reminded that the Jonadabs of the world are out there, just waiting to take advantage of others to help themselves.

At the end of 2 Samuel 13, David has stopped mourning for Amnon. Amnon is dead, and no degree of mourning will bring him back. Instead, David longs for Absalom. The text reads: "The heart of the king went out, yearning for Absalom." Perhaps David could not help the way he loved Absalom, but Absalom may have realized his father's feelings and used them to his own gain. It might be possible to love too much and to become blind to the way that love can be abused. The chapter ends with a kind of foreshadowing that we have not heard the last from Absalom and that David's family problems are far from being over.

Anti-heroes/Negative Role Models

The Old Testament does an excellent job of passing on the best human values and the best examples of godliness through hero stories or stories featuring positive role models. A young boy could read the stories of Joseph or Daniel and gain many positive insights. Young girls could emulate the stories of Esther, Ruth, or Deborah.

Similarly, the Old Testament provides examples of behaviors that are to be avoided rather than copied. Young people could learn as much from the tragic, negative role models of Samson, Lot, Cain, or Saul as they could the heroic Joseph, Daniel, or Esther.

> What do the activities of David's family members reveal about the way persons should not relate to one another in a family?

As the writer of Second Samuel describes David and the problems of his family, it is almost as if an entire nest of anti-heroes is being exposed. Here is a guidebook for how not to have a successful family. Where have you seen or experienced such negative behaviors in modern families? What do the activities of David's family members reveal about the way persons should not relate to one another in a family?

Priority on Family

First Timothy 5:8 makes a powerful, uncompromising statement: "Whoever does not provide for relatives, and especially for family members, has denied the faith and is worse than an unbeliever." This verse captures perfectly the priority that the ancient Jewish world placed on family that passed directly into the core of the Christian proclamation.

The story of David in Second Samuel becomes a powerful illustration of what goes wrong when family is given less than first priority. We know where David was in the construction of one of the greatest small empires in the ancient world; but where was he in giving attention to the needs of

> To what extent should the church be creating agendas that would restore focus on the family?

raising children and maintaining a family? Was he always at the office? Did he always have what appeared to be "more pressing matters"?

Most people would readily agree that the major problems of modern civilization can be traced to the breakdown of the traditional family unit. We realize this, but are there any real indications that people are doing much about it? To what extent should the church be creating agendas that would restore focus on the family? If we have "lost our way," as so many social commentators suggest, can this "way" be reclaimed by placing the priority on family?

Real People

The power of the Book of Second Samuel comes from the fact that it portrays human life exactly like it sometimes is. The book is frank and honest, and discussions of it must be equally frank.

Although Tamar was raped by Amnon, the story may remind us as well of experiences with other forms of sexual intimacy that do not involve rape. As soon as the sexual act was finished, Amnon was through with Tamar. All he wanted was the sex, and then he responded to her with violent rejection. How often every kind of promise imaginable, every devious argument, every type of attention is used to convince someone to be intimate. Then, after the intimacy is accomplished, the attention-giving, manipulating person disappears.

> As important as human sexuality is, it cannot be allowed to become the primary focus of a relationship.

As important as human sexuality is, it cannot be allowed to become the primary focus of a relationship. If a person gives obsessive attention to sexual activity, it is likely that once that activity takes place the relationship will become less rather than more. Amnon and Tamar clearly remind us that the activities of human sexual interaction must be pursued with tremendous care. Sex gone wrong usually leads to the most disastrous consequences.

Love Gone Wrong

Just as loving can go wrong in situations like Amnon's rape of Tamar, and even in Absalom's loving his sister so much that he was compelled to vicious revenge, loving can also go wrong when it is apparently wholesome and well-meaning. David loved Absalom with a deep intensity. No matter how far Absalom went in his rebellious behaviors, David was always wanting him back and mourning his absence. True love does not simply let itself be used and taken advantage of. To do so

> True love does not simply let itself be used and taken advantage of. To do so hurts the objects of a person's love more than it ever helps them.

hurts the objects of a person's love more than it ever helps them.

Why would David literally let Absalom and his other sons "get away with murder"? Is it possible that this was his way of making up to his children the lack of time and attention he had given them as they were growing up?

Because of his own failure with Bathsheba, was

David's ability to advise his children and criticize their activities made impossible? If our children think that our advice is hypocritical because of our past activities, is it likely that our advice can ever find credibility in their eyes?

Dimension 4:
A Daily Bible Journey Plan

Day 1: 2 Samuel 14:1-24

Day 2: 2 Samuel 14:25-33

Day 3: 2 Samuel 15:1-12

Day 4: 2 Samuel 15:13-29

Day 5: 2 Samuel 15:30-37

Day 6: 2 Samuel 16:1-14

Day 7: 2 Samuel 16:15-23

**2 Samuel
15:1-31;
18:1-15, 33**

12

ABSALOM, ABSALOM!

What to Watch For

William Faulkner's brother, Dean, died in an airplane crash in 1935.
Faulkner had bought the plane. The next year he wrote the novel,
Absalom, Absalom! The book, in part, reflects the agony and grief that
Faulkner was experiencing in his life, an emotional turmoil much like that
found in David's passionate sorrow for his errant son.

   Read 2 Samuel 15:1-31; 18:1-15, 33. In fact, it would help to read
Chapters 13–18 in their entirety. Try to determine in your reading how
Absalom could possibly dislodge David from the throne of Israel. Was not
David the idealized hero of heroes, beloved by all the people? Something
must have been happening behind the scenes, some flaw in David, that
made Absalom's uprising almost successful.

Dimension 1:
What Does the Bible Say?

1. What was the flaw in David's government that gave Absalom an opening for establishing his power? (2 Samuel 15:1-6)

2. Why did David abandon the city of Jerusalem? (2 Samuel 15:13-16)

3. Who was Ahithophel, and why would he probably have sided with Absalom? (2 Samuel 15:12; also see 2 Samuel 11:3; 23:34; 16:23)

4. How does David's attitude toward Absalom never change?

Dimension 2:
What Does the Bible Mean?

SETTING THE STAGE

For three years Absalom was in self-imposed exile following his successful plot to kill Amnon and to avenge Tamar. Not only was Absalom safe in Geshur (GESH-uhr), where his grandfather was king, but without question he was beginning to build his own political base there. The kingdom of Geshur had been defeated by David, and there was no great love among the Geshurites for the fabled Hebrew king. For Absalom, it was a starting point, like a hopeful presidential candidate winning the New Hampshire primary.

David's army commander and closest confidant, Joab, saw David's misery over Absalom's absence. He also knew that Absalom was, in fact, now heir to the throne. Joab took it upon himself to engineer a series of events that brought about Absalom's return to Jerusalem; but for two years David would not welcome him to the king's house. It can be assumed that Absalom used this time wisely to build his own following.

Finally, after this time had passed, Absalom took his own initiative. He sent for Joab, but Joab did not come. He sent a second time and was still refused. Absalom then instructed his servants to set Joab's barley field on

---

95

fire. This time Joab came. In a scene that is almost comical, Joab asks: "Why have your servants set my field on fire?" Absalom calmly responds: "I sent word to you."

Absalom decided to risk approaching David himself, opening himself to the possibility of David's revenge for Amnon's death or his father's utter rejection. In a moment reflective of Jesus' parable of the prodigal son, Absalom faced his father and prostrated himself on the ground; and David picked him up and kissed him. Absalom was back.

Chapter 15 describes Absalom's actions over the four years following his return to Jerusalem. Every day, first thing in the morning, he would station himself near the entrance to the king's house. People would line up to see the king in order to gain his advice or to have some legal matter settled. The king was not only a ruler and leader in battle—David's expertise—but also the final word of judgment in even the smallest disputes between people. Recall how the two women came to Solomon to settle the argument over who the mother of a small infant was (1 Kings 3:16-28). Such a matter might seem trite compared to the grand issues of national and international politics; but from the perspective of the common person on the street, making these kinds of day-to-day decisions was a primary function of kingship.

> David, Saul, and Solomon all committed the fatal flaw of becoming too far removed from the lives of the masses. When a ruler removes himself or herself from the people, his or her rule is made most vulnerable.

Evidently, David committed the fatal flaw that has plagued rulers across the ages. He allowed his rule to get too far removed from the lives of the masses. Saul at first had taken his court into the countryside where he dispensed judgment while seated under a shade tree. Then he withdrew and divided himself from the people behind walls of royalty. Solomon, in the early part of his reign, was almost totally accessible; but then the glamorous trappings of international politics distracted him from the basic needs of his people. When a ruler removes himself or herself from the people, his or her rule is made most vulnerable.

Absalom turned David's withdrawal from the people to his advantage. As he stood near the gate to the king's house, he stopped would-be petitioners. He explained how their claims would be ignored by an inefficient and uncaring government. However, Absalom personally would settle their cases and respond to their needs. That this process could go on for four years without David intervening shows how totally distracted David had become by more "lofty" matters. The people began to feel that their king did not care—but Absalom did. His power in the ranks of the people grew daily.

Absalom then appealed to David for permission to go to Hebron (HEE-bruhn) to worship God at the sanctuary there. Perhaps David should have been suspicious. Could fully satisfactory worship not occur in Jerusalem? When David told his son, "Go in peace," he may have been implying more than simply, "Have a good time, see you later." He may have sensed some special need to appease a man who was gaining tremendous power. He may have been expressing a desire that peace continue to exist between them.

Hebron had its own power. It had once been the capital of Israel, but David had taken that honor and prestige away. The strong leadership of the city and its surrounding area of influence was anything but pro-David. Absalom knew this. He was not going to Hebron to pray but rather to continue his grand scheme for gaining power. Perhaps Absalom did not trust that being crown prince

> Absalom withdrew to Hebron, an area of influence that was anything but pro-David, to continue his grand scheme for gaining power.

guaranteed his succession to the throne. Perhaps he saw the favor of David turning toward another son, Solomon. Perhaps he simply did not want to wait. Absalom sent secret messengers throughout Israel informing a broad range of followers that he would be made king at Hebron and then would march on Jerusalem. His well-conceived conspiracy was about to explode across all Palestine.

A wise advisor named Ahithophel (uh-HITH-uh-fel) followed Absalom and offered his counsel and leadership. Ahithophel had once stood at the center of David's court. Why would he show such disloyalty? He may have seen in Absalom the next leader of Israel and wanted to secure his political position. He may have disliked the failure of David's government. Even more, there may have been revenge in Ahithophel's heart; he was Bathsheba's grandfather and may still have burned within over the dishonor that David had brought to his household. The implications of the old sin may have risen again.

When word of the advance of Absalom's forces on Jerusalem reached David, he immediately fled the city with all his household. It is not clear why David would have done this. Fighting a defensive battle from within the walls of a fortified city would have seemed much more sensible. However, David, forever the military genius, may have been more comfortable organizing guerilla, offensive warfare in the country-side. Even more, he may have had to get out of

> David may have had to leave Jerusalem in order to see who would follow him.

the city to see who would follow him. In his distancing himself from the people, he may not have known whom he could trust in Jerusalem. The

Listening to the wrong advisor led to Absalom's defeat and death.

ark of the covenant was removed with David, but he had it returned to Jerusalem. If it was the will of God that he remain king, David would return and renew his worship before the ark at Jerusalem.

Absalom occupied Jerusalem and probably had the momentum needed to rout David and to make himself king. Ahithophel gave excellent advice that David should be pursued immediately while he was on the run and his forces still disorganized. Another advisor, Hushai (HOOSH-igh), who had remained loyal to David, went to Absalom. Absalom repected his wisdom, believed that he also had changed loyalties, and sought his advice. Hushai counseled a delay so that better organization and strategy could take place on Absalom's part. Absalom followed Hushai's plan rather than that of Ahithophel. The choice was disastrous in its effect, as David gained the time needed to reorganize a powerful army of his own.

A great battle was engaged in the forest of Ephraim. Military historians might be reminded of the Argonne forest in France where the United States forces brought massive defeat on the Germans in World War I, the Ardennes forest where the famed "Battle of the Bulge" took place in the bitter winter of 1944, or the woods at Chickamauga where more than 34,000 soldiers were killed, wounded, or captured in less than two days' fighting during the American Civil War. The forest was David's turf. When Absalom's armies came, they were destroyed.

Even as David's armies marched toward the forest, the king specifically compelled his commanders to "deal gently" with Absalom. Second Samuel 18:5 stresses that "all the people" were witnesses to David's command. But then Joab (JOH-ab), the commander, took matters into his own hands. He refused to let David accompany the army so that he could not become a possible trophy that would inspire Absalom's soldiers.

David ordered his commanders to "deal gently" with Absalom. But Joab took matters into his own hands.

In the midst of the battle Absalom, who was riding on his mule—the primary means of royal transportation—caught his head in the fork of a tree. While Absalom dangled beneath the tree, Joab pierced his heart with three spears. Absalom was still alive, so ten young soldiers surrounded him and slaughtered him unmercifully. Perhaps the youth of the soldiers is emphasized to show that a new generation had now arrived in Israel that knew little of the traditions and personality that were David's. Absalom's end was horrific.

David, "sitting between the two gates" (2 Samuel 18:24), was anxiously awaiting word of the battle. But, when the messenger comes from Joab with the news of battle, David is not so much concerned about the victory in battle. Instead, he asks: "Is it well with the young man Absalom?"

(18:29, 32). With the news of his son's death, pent-up emotion erupts in deepest misery: "O my son Absalom, my son, my son Absalom! Would I had died instead of you, O Absalom, my son, my son!" (18:33).

David had become a shadow of his former self. He was broken and distraught, but almost certainly the demands of kingship had not drained his life of its energy and strength. Rather, he had watched his family destroy itself; and when the destruction began to come, it was too late for David to change its course.

> David was broken and distraught watching the destruction of his family. When David had his chance to make a difference, he had been absent and neglected that which was most important. Now, it was too late.

When David had his chance to make a difference, he had been absent and neglected that which was most important. Now, it was too late. In his heart he knew this, and it destroyed him.

Dimension 3: What Does the Bible Mean to Us?

A Political Warning

Abraham Lincoln, in his "Gettysburg Address," pledged to dedicate himself to seeing that "government of the people, by the people, for the people, shall not perish from the earth." The great kings of Israel's United Kingdom, Saul, David, and Solomon, did not share the same dedication. They began as kings of the people, for the people, and from the people. Soon, though, supposedly grander agendas clouded their vision of what was most important. Basic needs of the common citizen got lost, and with this loss loyalty and support from the masses disappeared.

Absalom was an absolutely smart politician. It may even be possible that part of his turn to the people was motivated by the incompetence and mediocrity he saw in David's government. Some people might even be able to make a good case for Absalom's revolt. Could he have been a legitimate reformer? If you had been a common citizen of Jerusalem, how might you have responded to Absalom? The terribly negative view of Absalom in Second Samuel certainly reflects the perspective of those highly loyal to David.

> Many citizens today, as may have those of David's day, complain that their government has gotten too big, that it is consumed with such high profile issues in international and domestic politics that the daily life needs of the common person get lost.

Could modern governments take a lesson from this section of Scripture? There seems to be a great outcry on the part of many citizens that their government has gotten too big, that it is consumed with such high profile issues in international and domestic politics that the daily life needs of the common person get lost. Nations become ripe for turmoil and even revolution when conditions like those in the days of David and Absalom persist.

David's Dismay

David was at his best when military action was required. Even as he was fleeing Jerusalem and confusion reigned, he was able to rally his troops, delegate authority, and create a successful battle plan.

> Is it possible that the real problem with Davidic Israel was much deeper than government? If the true basis for human civilization—family—is diminished, is it likely that other social structures can be sustained?

Yet, when family crises occurred, the strong king suddenly became all but emotionally incapable of any positive action. In all the stories about the decline of his family, he never moves to act decisively in a way that will possibly bring about a resolution of the problems.

How is it possible for a person to be so capable in a work arena and yet so inept in a family environment? What would the evolution of this lack of ability in family matters have been like over the years? Might David have gotten help and changed his direction? What form might this "help" have taken? At some point did it become "too late" to seek help?

Modern families should study closely the decline of David's family. What appear as the priorities of David's life can be seen at the heart of the difficulties of many modern families. The terrible end for David and all these people he undoubtedly loved may be viewed as prophetic.

Eventually, David's government began to fail. Is it possible that the real problem with Davidic Israel was much deeper than government? If the true basis for human civilization—family—is diminished, is it likely that other social structures can be sustained?

A Poverty of Listening

Throughout the dismal story of David's family some of the poorest listening in any historical record is encountered. Amnon listens to Jonadab and calamity reigns. Absalom listens to Hushai and loses the opportunity for victory. Joab does not listen to David, and Absalom is killed. David evidently fails to listen to Nathan and continues to neglect his family. No one in the government seems to be listening to the people, and they are ready for revolution. Worst of all, there is no evidence of anyone listening to God.

A full range of problems in modern society are caused by poor communication skills. Think about the number of interpersonal and business relationships that fail because of a failure to communicate. Those immortal lines from the Paul Newman movie "Cool Hand Luke" are prophetic for the modern age: "What we've got here is failure to communicate."

We must remember that a major factor in good communication is good listening. Most people could greatly profit from some kind of training in listening skills. What might such training involve? The world that the writer of Second Samuel described was a world consumed with busy-ness. It was a world in which people became too busy to listen well. The wrong voices prevailed at the wrong times, and there was disaster. And again—no one seemed to be listening to God.

> A major factor in good communication is good listening. The world that the writer of Second Samuel described was a world consumed with busy-ness; the wrong voices prevailed at the wrong times, and there was disaster. And—no one seemed to be listening to God.

Love Never Ends

From the beginning of the Bible until its end, the unrelenting love of God is proclaimed again and again. God's love directed God's actions in the days of Noah and at Sodom and Gomorrah. Jesus came because "God so loved the world." Paul described love that never ends in 1 Corinthians 13 and asserted in Romans 8 that absolutely nothing can separate us from the love of God.

David epitomizes and embodies a god-like love that never ends. Absalom went contrary to David's will in almost every way imaginable. Absalom even rose to destroy the very force that had given him life and opportunity. But through it all, one thing remained constant: David never ceased to love his son. The parallel is striking: God, in love, never stops being for humans. In spite of whatever humans might do, how far off track our lives might go, God's love is still there to the end and—as in Absalom's case—beyond the end.

Dimension 4:
A Daily Bible Journey Plan

Day 1: **2 Samuel 17:1-14**

Day 2: **2 Samuel 17:15-29**

Day 3: **2 Samuel 18:1-18**

Day 4: **2 Samuel 18:19-32**

Day 5: **2 Samuel 18:33–19:15**

Day 6: **2 Samuel 19:16-30**

Day 7: **2 Samuel 19:31-43**

13

CENSUS, PLAGUE, AND SACRIFICE

What to Watch For

The Book of Second Samuel ends with a random collection of materials that complete the story of David and make way for a transition to the rule of Solomon after David's death. Read 2 Samuel 19–24. Note that there was one more small rebellion following that of Absalom. Chapter 22 is a long poetic section in which David praises and thanks God for his triumph over the Philistines. Another poetic section (23:1-7) is termed "David's last words." A listing of leading figures in the war against the Philistines is included at 23:8-39. The list could have been compiled for some sort of pension-like purpose for these men or their families. Interestingly, Uriah the Hittite, Bathsheba's first husband, is included in the list (verse 39). The census, focused on in the final chapter, represents a last calamity for David's government.

Dimension 1: What Does the Bible Say?

1. What did David tell Joab to do? How long did it take? (2 Samuel 24:2, 8)

2. How did David feel after taking the census? (2 Samuel 24:10)

3. With what three choices was David presented? (2 Samuel 24:11-13)

4. Where did the pestilence sent by the Lord end? (2 Samuel 24:16)

Dimension 2:
What Does the Bible Mean?

SETTING THE STAGE

How much David's hopes and dreams for Israel under his leadership must have seemed to be coming unravelled in the latter stages of his life. Absalom's revolt and death shook him to the core of his existence. For a moment, the entire enterprise was almost lost in confusion. Had it not been for Joab's strong hand, there is no telling what might have happened.

Slowly the nation began to come together again. A rather insignificant uprising was put down, David pulled himself out of his personal malaise, and the people decided that he still was their best opportunity for leadership. There was a common mourning for Absalom, and surely those leaders under David had to realize that Absalom had established a strong following in Israel. The Davidic leaders really needed to listen to what Absalom's support and following had meant.

Absalom wanted to return government a little closer to the people and their daily needs. Government probably needed to be "downsized," to use a modern term. It needed to be less expensive, less demanding, and infinitely more accessible. Israel's world was back to peace, agreement, and stability again. Whatever next steps might be taken would have to be taken with great caution. It was no time for mistaken judgment.

At the beginning of 2 Samuel 24 David orders a census. Typically, a census was used for two primary purposes. First, and this seems to be the situation in Second Samuel, a census could be used to determine the number of men available for war. The census was like a tabulation that would precede a draft or a major call to arms. Second, the census could be used as a preliminary step in a taxation process. The census that brought Mary and Joseph to Bethlehem was an initial part of the process of Roman taxation in first-century Palestine.

Both of these possibilities—draft and taxation—were movements of a government that wanted more control and more domination of people's lives, not the lessening of power that Absalom had stood for and the people found so appealing. The census was the tool of a heavy-handed, more centralized government, the kind of government that totally cut against the grain of the independence and autonomy that was at the core of the Hebrew spirit.

Even more, a highly centralized government did not seem to be the will of God. The more that people placed their faith in government, the less they held to their faith in God. Raise a lot of money, field a mighty army, and success and safety would be assured. Such thinking was not religious thinking. These were highly secular ideas. If trust was really in God, such movements of human government would not be demanded.

> A highly centralized government did not seem to be the will of God. The more that people placed their faith in government, the less they held to their faith in God.

The problem at the end of David's government is the same problem that Israel faced during the time of the prophet Isaiah. A huge debate raged in Isaiah's day. Should Israel side with Egypt or side with Assyria? For Isaiah, there was but one choice—side with God. Isaiah's very name meant "in Yahweh/God there is salvation," not in Egypt and not in Assyria. David needed to understand, especially after all the events involving Absalom, that the salvation of Israel was not to be found in more controlling, more secular government.

Who was David listening to? Certainly not Joab and his army commanders. Joab's advice had been right on target. He had literally saved David's kingship. Now, David was listening to someone else. In all likelihood, the people who would have profited from larger government had his ear. Maybe David was influenced by his own lobbyists and special interest groups. Without question, there would have been those who would profit greatly from a major, expansionistic war effort or who would find ways to transfer large tax monies into their own pockets.

> Who was David listening to? Joab's advice had been right on target, and he tried to get David to listen; but David refused. When David finally had a change of heart, it was too late.

105

Joab and his commanders tried to get David to listen, but David refused. Loyal Joab then went throughout the land and carried out the will of his king. As soon as the census was complete, however, David had a change of heart. He "was stricken to the heart," and he felt that he had sinned against God and the people. Why David changed his opinion is not clear. Perhaps a groundswell of disgust with the census and his reign began to make David feel vulnerable. David may have been moving quickly to cover his own tracks before word of revolution began to rise again.

> God was clearly displeased by David taking the census. In fact, the writer of First Chronicles credits Satan with initiating the census.

The text seems confused about God's role in the census. Clearly, it is all in opposition to God's will and brings about God's greatest displeasure. Yet, the first verse of Chapter 24 gives God credit for initiating the census. Based on God's later response, this first verse makes no sense. In fact, by the time the Chronicler wrote his history of Israel credit—or blame—for the census was given to Satan (1 Chronicles 21:1). In all likelihood, the idea that God initiated the census may have come from persons within David's inner circle who gave the census greater credibility by claiming that God was behind it. Beyond question, God was not.

David cried out to God for forgiveness, a process he repeated over and over again in his life. Often, this forgiveness had come fairly easily and almost immediately. This time, however, there would be no simplicity of forgiveness. Instead, a prophet named Gad came with a message of punishment. The Bible gives little information about the prophet Gad. He is peripherally involved in David's reign, appearing only at random moments. Gad is credited with being instrumental in establishing the religious order of temple managers, the Levites (2 Chronicles 29:25).

David must choose between three years of famine, three months of pursuit by an enemy, or three days of pestilence. Three years of famine was too long, and what "pestilence" meant was not made clear. David was certain he did not want to ever be pursued by an enemy again, even if it was only for three months. He decided to "fall" into the mercy of God rather than the hands of enemies and chose to accept whatever pestilence might mean. Perhaps he should have asked for a clarification. Three days of pestilence resulted in the death of seventy thousand people. A truly unselfish person would have chosen being pursued by an enemy; this choice would not have brought great harm to others. David finally begged God to punish him and his household, not these innocent people.

An angel of destruction appeared as God's vehicle of punishment. In the standard thinking of that day and time, angels were helpers of God who could be used in this way. The Bible gives no detailed explanation about angels. They were accepted as a given, as was the idea that God easily used natural events to bring about punishment. In addition, there was an under-standing that God could stop the movement of punishment at any moment.

When the pestilence stopped, the point of its advance through the city of Jerusalem was the threshing floor of Araunah (uh-RAW-nuh). Great events were not required to make a spot take on an air of special holiness, so something like a pestilence stopping its spread at Araunah's threshing floor certainly would make that spot especially holy.

David built an altar on the spot, and Araunah gave the oxen used in the threshing as animals to be offered on the altar. The threshing equipment itself was used as fuel. David insisted on paying for what Araunah had given. That David insisted on paying may indicate that he was, indeed, con-cerned about the common people, the "sheep" of verse 17. Under most circumstances, a king would simply "appropriate" the belongings of someone else without any concern for that person being paid back.

> David built an altar to God on the spot where the pestilence ended—the site where Solomon would build the Temple of God on Mount Moriah.

The altar area at the threshing floor took on even greater significance under Solomon's kingship. Araunah's threshing floor became the site where Solomon would build the Temple of God on Mount Moriah (2 Chronicles 3:1).

Second Samuel is now complete. David has been king for forty years, reigning seven years at Hebron and thirty-three years at Jerusalem. The land for the Temple is ready for the appearance of a temple-builder, a new king who will move Israel beyond the era of David. Solomon is waiting in the wings preparing to move to center stage.

Dimension 3:
What Does the Bible Mean to Us?

When Will They Ever Learn?

Featured in the counterculture music of the 1960's was a war protest song entitled "Where Have All the Flowers Gone?" The answer to the question raised by the song was graveyards, graveyards filled with soldiers whose lives had been lost in yet another misadventure of human folly. The com-pelling refain of the song asked: "When will they ever learn? When will they ever learn?"

Why do people keep making the same mistakes over and over again, even after they have seen the horrible implications of those mistakes? For David to push the idea of a census just when Israel was

> Why do people keep making the same mistakes over and over again?

beginning to gain stability again makes no sense at all. Most of the time, you think that people will act in their own best interests. How can people become as nearly self-destructive as David was? In what other situations do people act equally as foolishly? Why? Determine why David took the census, and you probably will discover decisively valuable insights into the inner workings of human nature.

Making Things Right

With his "stricken" heart, which probably came more from necessity than desire, David may have hoped for an easy forgiveness and restoration into God's favor. Who would not want "making things right" to be easy?

> Only when we accept responsibility for our actions and embrace the pain of those actions in our life can we expect turnarounds to be possible.

However, this time restoration of his relationship with God would be painfully difficult. David tried to pass the pain off to others at first, and then only as he accepted responsibility and asked that the pain be directed at him did any real resolution begin.

There is an important lesson here: only when we accept responsibility for our actions and embrace the pain of those actions in our life can we expect turnarounds to be possible. We must also wait at times over long periods of painful healing for resolution of trouble to take place. David's pestilence illustrates clearly that punishment and forgiveness are not always easy processes.

God and Natural Calamity

People have drawn conclusions based on the information available to them at a particular time and the conditioning of their traditional beliefs that may not be accurate. For example, think about the way in which ancient people thought that the world was flat or that the earth was at the center of what we now know is actually a solar/sun-centered system. People were thinking the best they knew how, but they were still wrong.

Theology could be as mistaken in its primitive formulations as science was. Some early understandings of God have not stood the long test of time, and revisions have had to be considered.

In the world of the writer of Second Samuel, a connection was always made between natural calamities and the will of God. Not only did God's will allow for natural calamities but God created and used these calamities as sources of punishment for people who had done wrong.

Has this kind of thinking stood the test of time, or is it clear that God does not act in these ways? How might it affect our thinking about God if earthquakes, snow storms, hurricanes, or lightning fires are seen as God's way of punishing evil? What if you were indeed a good person and got caught up in such "natural" disasters? Might substantial conflicts about

God rise in your mind if, in the integrity of your character, you knew you had not done anything deserving such punishment?

The Book of Job signals a new level of thinking in Israel that moved beyond the old traditional conclusions. The conclusion of the Book of Job is that bad things can happen to good people simply because bad things are part of the mix of life. There is no need to attach a theological explanation. Jesus moved in the direction of this same sort of new thinking when he stressed that the sun rises on both the good and the evil and the rain falls on both the just and the unjust (Matthew 5:45b). Understandings of God evolve over time. The God of pestilence with the angel of death is representative of an early understanding. The understanding is not wrong; it is simply early.

> Jesus stressed that the sun rises on both the good and the evil and the rain falls on both the just and the unjust.

A True Picture

The writer of the two books of Samuel has done us a great favor. Some ancient literature depicts heroic figures as having lives that are flawless and above error. In Egypt, for example, negative information was often totally omitted from their recorded histories. While heroic characters, intentions, and actions certainly make up part of the Samuel history, these heroes struggle with real problems and sometimes do not do very well in their struggles. David was indeed a hero, but David had weaknesses common to all humanity.

It is important to see David at his best. It is equally important to see him at his worst. The lessons we gain from his poor performance as a father in a family are invaluable. Every husband and father—every parent—should have Second Samuel as required reading. The follies of giving one's life to one's job or neglecting family in order to pursue profession are presented with striking clarity.

> Every husband and father—every parent—should have Second Samuel as required reading.

Part of the profundity of the Bible is the way in which it gives an accurate picture of the human condition. The full range of potential, from the best to the worst, is openly acknowledged. The portrait of David drawn in First and Second Samuel is masterful in every way. If the lessons of these books are taken to heart, human relationships that we find ourselves caught up in daily cannot help but be enhanced.

Dimension 4:
A Daily Bible Journey Plan

Day 1: 2 Samuel 20

Day 2: 2 Samuel 21:1-14

Day 3: 2 Samuel 21:15-22

Day 4: 2 Samuel 22:1-25

Day 5: 2 Samuel 22:26-51

Day 6: 2 Samuel 23

Day 7: 2 Samuel 24

GLOSSARY

Absalom (AB-suh-luhm)—Son of David and brother of Tamar. Had his half brother Amnon killed. Rebelled against his father. Killed in battle, which deeply grieved David.

Amnon (AM-non)—Son of David. Dishonored his half sister Tamar and was killed at the command of her full brother Absalom as a result.

Bathsheba (bath-SHEE-buh)—Wife of Uriah the Hittite, whom David had killed in order to marry her. Mother of Solomon.

Bethel (BETH-uhl)—A town of Palestine, eleven miles north of Jerusalem. One of the cities on Samuel's circuit.

David (DAY-vid)—Israel's greatest king. Native of Bethlehem. Served under Saul. Anointed king by Samuel. United northern and southern tribes and put capital at Jerusalem.

Eli (EE-ligh)—Priest and judge of Israel for forty years. He trained the young Samuel.

En-gedi (en-GED-igh)—An oasis in the wilderness area west of the Dead Sea, about thirty-five miles southeast of Jerusalem. David spared Saul's life in a nearby cave.

Gilgal (GIL-gal)—Site near Jericho where Saul was made king. One of the cities on Samuel's circuit.

Goliath (guh-LIGH-uhth)—The Philistine "champion of Gath," a giant who fought and was defeated by the young David.

Hannah (HAN-uh)—Wife of Elkanah (el-KAY-nuh) and mother of Samuel.

Hebron (HEE-bruhn)—City in southern Palestine in the territory of the tribe of Judah. David's first capital.

Jerusalem (ji-ROO-suh-luhm)—City chosen by David as capital of United Kingdom. Located on a tableland on the crest of the central ridge of Palestine.

Joab (JOH-ab)—David's nephew. Commander of David's army.

Helped kill David's rebellious son, Absalom.

Jonathan (JON-uh-thuhn)— Eldest son of King Saul. Friend of David.

Michal (MIGH-kuhl)—King Saul's daughter. David's first wife.

Mizpah (MIZ-puh)—A town in the area of the tribe of Benjamin. One of the cities on Samuel's circuit.

Nathan (NAY-thuhn)—Prophet during the reigns of David and Solomon. Advised David not to build a temple. Made David aware of his sin with Bathsheba.

Philistines (fi-LIS-teenz)—People of Philistia on eastern coast of Mediterranean. Controlled cities of Gaza, Ashkelon, Ashdod, Ekron, and Gath. Enemies of Israel at time of conquest and judges. Saul and Jonathan defeated them. David repelled invasions of the Philistines.

Samuel (SAM-yoo-uhl)—First Hebrew prophet after Moses and last of the judges. Raised in the sanctuary at Shiloh by Eli, he anointed Saul the first king of Israel. When Saul was rejected by God, Samuel anointed David.

Saul (sawl)—First king of Israel. Anointed by Samuel; he was rejected by God when he made an unlawful sacrifice. When David was anointed to replace him, Saul tried to kill him. Eventually Saul was killed by the Philistines.

Tamar (TAY-mahr)—Daughter of David and sister of Absalom who was violated by her half brother Amnon.

Uriah (yoo-RIGH-uh)—A Hittite, Bathsheba's husband, member of David's army, whom David had killed to prevent discovery of his infidelity with Bathsheba.